An Introduction to Malawi: Basic Facts

Cecilia Lawrence

Copyright (c) 2017 Cecilia Lawrence
All rights reserved.

An Introduction to Malawi: Basic Facts
Cecilia Lawrence

First Edition

ISBN-13: 9781979972772
ISBN-10: 197997277X

CreateSpace
Scotts Valley, California, USA

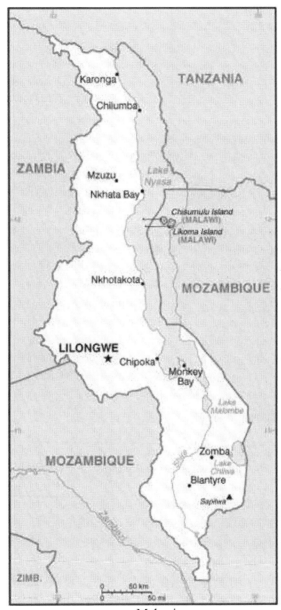

Malawi

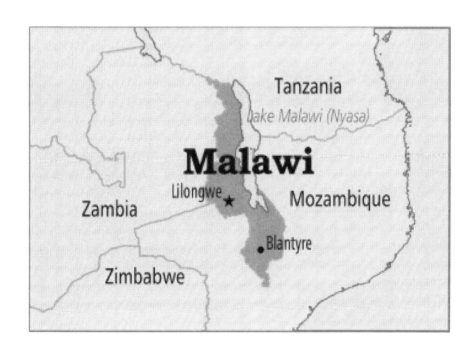

Introduction

THIS WORK provides basic facts about Malawi. It is intended to serve as a brief introduction to this southeast African country and enable some people, who know nothing or very little about Malawi, to learn important facts which can help them learn more about the people and the history of one of the most fascinating countries on the African continent.

I have also written about Malawi in my other works, *The Countries of Southern Africa* and *Life in Southern Africa*.

I deliberately made this book short and small for those reasons instead of providing a lot of details on the subjects I have covered concerning the people, the history and the land of Malawi.

Who are people of Malawi? What are their ethnic identities? What is the country's history? How is the land? What are some of its prominent features? How is life in Malawi? What are some of the cultural aspects which give the country its own identity? Is there a national culture or simply cultures of different ethnic groups?

What are some of the towns and cities of this predominantly agricultural country and one of the poorest in Africa?

What is the country's future in a region with richer and more powerful neighbours? Is federation with them possible and a solution to the country's economic problems?

Those are some of the questions I have attempted to answer in this book. They are also some of the questions, and many others, which can be answered by doing more research on the country, a task beyond the scope of this work which is meant to be no more than a simple introduction to a country that is known as "The Warm Heart of Africa."

You will be heartened to learn more than you have from this simple introduction to Malawi.

Welcome to Malawi.

General Background

MALAWI is located in East Africa. But it is usually not considered to be an East African country like Kenya, Uganda and Tanzania because it is located farther south. It is in the southeastern part of the continent and is considered to be an integral part of southern Africa.

Yet many Malawians known and say their country is in East Africa and is therefore an East African country. In fact, it is geographically more "East African" than Rwanda and Burundi which are far away from the East African coast unlike Malawi. Yet the twin states – Rwanda and Burundi – are considered to be East African and are members of the East African Community together with Tanzania, Uganda, Kenya and South Sudan.

Malawi is also an integral part of south-central Africa and was once a member of the Central African Federation during British colonial rule.

The federation was also known as the Federation of Rhodesia and Nyasaland. Malawi was then known as Nyasaland. It changed its name to Malawi after independence.

The federation was composed of Southern Rhodesia, now Zimbabwe; Northern Rhodesia, renamed Zambia; and Nyasaland.

Here is some background to the federation:

"In 1953, in the face of African opposition, Britain had consolidated the two colonies of Rhodesia with Nyasaland (now Malawi) in the ill-fated Federation of Rhodesia and Nyasaland, which was dominated by Southern Rhodesia. The Federation was established on August 1st 1953.

The Federation of Rhodesia and Nyasaland, also known as the Central African Federation (CAF), was a semi-independent federation of three southern African territories – the self-governing British colony of Southern Rhodesia and the British protectorates of Northern Rhodesia and Nyasaland – between 1953 and 1963.

Constitutionally, it was a federal realm of the British Crown, meaning that it was neither a Crown colony nor a dominion. As, however, the intention was that the federation would, in due course, become a dominion in the Commonwealth of Nations, the British sovereign ('the Crown') was represented by a Governor-General.

The Federation was established...with the aim of forging a middle way between a fully independent majority-ruled state and the white-dominated territory of South Africa. It was intended to be a permanent entity, but ultimately crumbled because the black African nationalists wanted a greater share of power than the dominant minority white population was willing to concede.

Northern Rhodesia had attracted a relatively small number of European settlers, but from the time these first secured political representation, they agitated for white minority rule, either as a separate entity or associated with Southern Rhodesia and possibly Nyasaland.

The mineral wealth of Northern Rhodesia made full amalgamation attractive to Southern Rhodesian politicians, but the British government preferred a looser association that included Nyasaland. This was intended to protect Africans in Northern Rhodesia and Nyasaland from discriminatory Southern Rhodesian laws.

The Federation of Rhodesia and Nyasaland...was intensely unpopular among the African majority and its formation hastened calls for majority rule.

It was commonly understood that Southern Rhodesia would be the dominant territory in the federation – economically, electorally, and militarily. How much so defined much of the lengthy constitutional negotiations and modifications that followed. African political opposition and nationalist aspirations, for the time, were mute.

Decisive factors in both the creation and dissolution of the Federation were the significant difference between the number of Africans and Europeans in the Federation, and the difference between the number of Europeans in Southern Rhodesia compared to the Northern Protectorates. Compounding this was the significant growth in Southern Rhodesia's European settler population (overwhelmingly British migrants), unlike in the Northern Protectorates. This was to greatly shape future developments in the Federation.

In 1939, approximately 60,000 Europeans resided in Southern Rhodesia; shortly before the Federation was established there were 135,000; by the time the Federation was dissolved they had reached 223,000 (though newcomers could only vote after three years of residency). Nyasaland showed the least European and greatest African population growth." "Rhodesia and Nyasaland," www.worldofcoins.eu/forum).

If the federation were formed today, it would be in the best interest of all the countries involved, unlike in the past when it was an instrument of domination by the white settlers to perpetuate imperial rule and exploit the indigenous people. As Nick Wright of the history department at Adelaide University in Australia (1975 – 1991) who was also the Malawi correspondent for *Africa Confidential* (2003 – 2010) stated in his article, "Central Africa's Sovereign Issues: Malawi, Zambia and Zimbabwe," in *African Arguments*, 5 August 2011:

"In March 2009, I wrote an article entitled "A New Federation" which suggested that Malawi may be moving slowly, and without anybody really noticing, towards the Federation which had been so firmly rejected by Hastings Banda of Malawi and Kenneth Kaunda of Zambia in the lead-up to Independence.

In the 1950s that was the Central African Federation of Northern and Southern Rhodesia, and Nyasaland, promoted by the British colonial power, and emphatically rejected by Banda and Kaunda on the very reasonable grounds that the white government of the regional super-power, Southern Rhodesia under Sir Roy Welensky, would seek to dominate it.

Not long after writing that article, I was in the Malawian capital, Lilongwe, seeking an interview with President Mutharika. His Press Secretary advised me, with every show of seriousness, to wait by the roadside to see the president's motorcade that would soon pass from Kamuzu International Airport to State House.

I often get into trouble for seeing humour where none was intended — and for missing the jokes when they do come — so I responded cautiously. Was this proposal, I silently wondered, an alternative to the interview I'd requested? Was he telling me not to anticipate the usual privileges that neo-colonial whites in Malawi had come to expect; to take my proper place in the stage-managed and bullying press conferences that local newsmen have to endure? Or was he trying to show me what an important person is the President of Malawi who merits such a long convoy?

I still do not know. At that time I took his meaning to be negative.

Suspicion of British "neo-colonialism" within Malawi played a strong part in the eventual collapse of the Federation, in 1962. By a curious irony, it is just such a suspicion within the governments of the successor states of Zimbabwe, Malawi and Zambia that today might impel them towards a revival of the Federation idea.

A generous, and remarkably "string-free", British aid policy during the post-independence period has been strongly condemned within Mugabe's circle of friends as an instrument of neo-colonialism . It is showing signs of collapse. It may have been the only thing preventing the formation of an economic federation in this region.

Why should these southern African states have surrendered the glories of their own sovereign status when nearly half of their national budgets were being paid-for by international aid donors (of which Britain was the most important)? Only the harsh economic realities of genuine independence could force their hands.

Natural ties between their peoples, together with their own political rhetoric, appear to be pushing these presidents towards the acceptance of that federation which was once anathema to their predecessors and a defining part of their anti-colonial credentials. But have they noticed it?

Recent events offer further encouragement for a reassessment of federalism in this southern African region. Anti-British sentiments are running higher than ever within the governments (though not, I think, the peoples) of all three former-members of the old Federation, fuelled constantly by Robert Mugabe's burning sense of grievance against Britain. The expulsion from Malawi of British High Commissioner, Fergus Cochrane-Dyet, for appearing to have criticised Mutharika in his mild diplomatic cables to London, is only the most recent of these events.

Sensitivity towards a largely illusory "neo-colonialism" may now become the catalyst for valuable political experimentation. If Malawi is to survive as an aid-free, state, as claimed recently by Mutharika, in a world in which British aid is no longer an automatic economic lifeline, it must begin by sharing some of its precious sovereignty with its neighbours. It must make haste to ally itself with neighbouring African states with which it has obvious affinities and complementary economies.

The Zambian President has already been accused of being a Malawian by parentage and a Zimbabwean in sentiment, and has countered with the accusation that the Opposition leader, Michael Sata, is more of a Tanzanian than a Zambian. Mutharika's first wife was Zimbabwean; he has property there and an admiring relationship with its President Mugabe. Many Malawians suspect that his sympathies are more Zimbabwean than Malawian.

But why all this language of old colonialism? Why *shouldn't* they feel as much at home in Zimbabwe, in Malawi and in Zambia? Malawi's dominant Chewa tribe belongs to all three of them and its major festival is in Zambia. Even the name which Zambia's current president shares with Malawi's first is a give-away.

As elsewhere in Africa, porous borders and economic realities have always hinted at the absurdity of tiny sovereignties within the old colonial boundaries of southern Africa. It is no insult to Malawi to suggest that it is a very poor country, and that it is poorer alone than as part of a collectivity. Malawians have always understood, when it comes to the important things in life — like selling off a tobacco crop at a good price, or finding a job — borders are things to be crossed.

Even President Mutharika of Malawi must realise that his visionary pet-project to construct an Indian Ocean port at Nsanje, three hundred kilometres from the sea, amidst the mudbanks of the Shire River, can only have some credibility if the other landlocked states of the old Federation get together on this.

If Bingu wants to go to sea on a regular basis from Nsanje, and to cross those hundreds of kilometres of Mozambican territory with cargoes of Malawian tobacco, tea and uranium for the world, he must really make haste to add some Zambian copper, and some Zimbabwean nickel and cheese, to that cargo.

Unfortunately, economic and international political realities rarely get the better of presidential hubris when it comes to flags, uniforms, palaces, private jets, VVIP suites, United Nations speeches, and, yes, presidential convoys. These things which make life so very enjoyable for today's presidents — and so inconvenient and annoying for everybody else — are too attractive to them. It is hard to think of a modern African presidency without these flummeries.

Could any of today's Zambian, Malawian and Zimbabwean presidents accept the logic of their own angry words against their former colonial power by surrendering some of their paper-thin sovereignties in favour of a workable union?

That will be a serious test for them."

They are all weak countries and will remain weak unless they unite to form a federation or even a confederation. Malawi is the weakest and poorest country in a region which would be strong if the countries were to unite and form one government.

Malawi also is one of the smallest countries in Africa in terms of area. But it is one of the most densely populated in the world.

It is a landlocked country, heavily dependent on Mozambique as an outlet to the sea. Access to the Indian Ocean is normally by rail to the port of Beira in the former Portuguese colony.

Malawi is bordered by Tanzania on the north and northeast; Mozambique on the east, south and southwest; and by Zambia on the west and northwest. It is separated from Tanzania and Mozambique by Lake Nyasa.

The lake has hundreds of fish species which are not found in any other part of the world. It is also one of the most prominent features of Malawi's identity. It is synonymous with Malawi. Without Lake Nyasa, Malawi would not be what it is today as a country.

Lake Nyasa is shared by Malawi, Tanzania and Mozambique. During the reign of Life-President Hastings Kamuzu Banda, Malawi claimed the entire lake and renamed it Lake Malawi. The claim was disputed by Tanzania. And the dispute continues today.

During colonial rule, both countries – which were then known as Nyasaland and Tanganyika – were ruled by the same colonial power: Britain. And all the maps during that period showed the boundary between the two countries ran in the middle of the lake. The lake was also known as Lake Nyasa, not Lake Malawi. Tanzanians still call it Lake Nyasa.

The maps were issued by the British colonial rulers. And they were used in government offices and in schools in Tanganyika and Nyasaland showing that both countries shared the lake.

Fortunately, the boundary dispute has not escalated into war. The two countries have enjoyed very good relations through the years since the end of Banda's reign. And because the dispute has not been resolved, it may be appropriate to continue calling the lake, Lake Nyasa as it was once known in both countries – Nyasaland and Tanganyika (now mainland Tanzania) – when they were ruled by the same colonial power.

One of the cardinal principles of the Organisation of African Unity (OAU) was to maintain borders inherited at independence. Both Malawi and Tanganyika were members of the OAU and now of the African Union (AU) which replaced the OAU. One country can not unilaterally redraw national boundaries.

One of the best ways to resolve the matter is unification. If Malawi and Tanzania unite under one government and form one country, the boundary between the two countries won't exist anymore. But that seems to be remote possibility. And historically, the two countries have never had strong ties until recently, especially since the mid- and late 1990s after the end of Banda's rule.

Banda was an Anglophile. Called *Ngwazi,* ("Fearless Warrior,") he was mesmerised by Britain.

He modelled his government on the British Parliament and built Kamuzu Academy as a private school patterned after Eton. Only the brightest and wealthiest were able to attend the academy; students were required to wear uniforms with straw boater hats and played cricket and rugby.

British influence is still strong in Malawi, clearly evident in the way the people dress and speak; how they drive – always on the left side of the road; in the existence of roundabouts in towns and speed bumps on roads; and the use of school uniforms.

Dr. Banda left an indelible mark on Malawi. The history of Malawi during the post-colonial era until his death was inextricably linked with his life.

With the fly whisk of a king and the homburg of a banker, Dr. Hastings Kamuzu Banda saw himself as the supreme ruler of Malawi – and he was. And it is almost impossible to understand post-colonial Nyasaland – renamed Malawi after independence – without knowing and understanding who Banda was. According to a report from Johannesburg, South Africa, entitled "Kamuzu Banda Dies; 'Big Man' Among Anticolonialists," in *The New York Times*, Thursday, November 27, 1997:

"Hastings Kamuzu Banda, a founding father in postcolonial Africa who led Malawi to independence in 1964 and then ruled it with a combination of caustic wit, eccentricity and cruelty for 30 years, died on Tuesday night in a hospital here.

Dr. Banda died of respiratory failure. He had been at the Garden City Clinic here for a week with pneumonia and fever after being transferred from a Malawian hospital. There is no record of his birth date; the clinic gave his age as 99, but Government documents during his rule would have made him about 90.

His longtime companion, Cecelia Kadzamira, was with him. She was giving updates on his condition, which apparently deteriorated after he seemed to be recovering two days ago. Many Malawians came to the hospital to wish him well, she said, and the Malawi Government had been very helpful.

That was no doubt a pleasant surprise: Dr. Banda generated mixed feelings among Malawians.

Many regarded him as the father of their nation, the former British Nyasaland, a Pennsylvania-sized splinter of land between Zambia and Mozambique. But after a revolt within his cabinet, he declared himself President for Life in 1971 and said his opponents would become 'food for crocodiles.'

Hundreds were killed, tortured or forced into exile -- and yet Malawi, which describes itself in tourist brochures as 'the warm heart of Africa,' managed to keep its reputation among Africans as a pocket of gentle-spirited people.

Dr. Banda was perhaps the most idiosyncratic of the 'big men' who led their countries out of colonialism. He held degrees from American and Scottish universities and his London medical offices became a sort of anticolonialist salon frequented by Jomo Kenyatta of Kenya and Kwame Nkrumah of the Gold Coast (now Ghana).

But once in power, Dr. Banda simultaneously affected the lion-tail fly whisk of an African king, the dark suits and homburgs of a British businessman and the arms of a Scottish baron. He refused to make speeches in African languages and established a school modeled on Eton in his birthplace, Mtunthama, where penniless students were taught Latin, Greek and African history from the British point of view. He hired only white foreigners to teach at the school and to run the ministries and businesses that built his personal fortune.

Under his rule, Malawi spurned black nationalist movements and was the only African nation with diplomatic ties to apartheid South Africa and to Israel.

He was the darling of cold warriors and big business, and amassed power in his own hands, keeping the Ministries of Justice, Foreign Affairs, Agriculture and Public works to himself, as well as the trusteeship of the state monopolies in tobacco farming, factories, oil and banking.

He was also the rector of the state university and the dominant figure in the local Presbyterian Church of Scotland.

He never married and said he had no children, but lived with Miss Kadzamira, his 'official hostess,' for 30 years. Victorian in his demands on public morality, he banned women from wearing pants or miniskirts. Long-haired male tourists arriving in Malawi either submitted to shearing by the airport barber or went home.

He also banned television, though he watched it himself by satellite, and prevented the Simon and Garfunkel song 'Cecelia' from being played on local radio, considering it an affront to his consort.

He referred to Malawi's 10 million citizens as 'my children' and was said to be deeply embittered when they turned him out in 1994.

There was always a Potemkin-village quality about his reign. Dr. Banda proudly claimed that Malawi was self-sufficient in food, but an annual ritual -- his visit to a field bursting with grain -- was carefully stage-managed in special fields seeded with hybrid plants artificially watered and fertilized. In fact, malnutrition was widespread by the late 1980's, with one child in five dying before the age of 5.

Such extraordinary suffering was a result partly of poor harvests, and partly of Government demands that peasants grow tobacco and other crops for export. One year, protesting farmers chopped down the model field he was to visit. Dr. Banda simply went to another.

His sleek capital, Lilongwe, was built with South

African money and South Africa underwrote and trained the red-shirted Young Pioneers, a paramilitary youth group that spied on citizens and terrorized dissidents.

And in one of the world's smallest and poorest nations, where the per-capita income was $200 a year, Dr. Banda kept five residences, a fleet of British luxury cars and a private jet.

Dr. Banda was born near the turn of the century of Chewa parents who named him Kamuzu -- Little Root -- because a shaman's root medicine apparently cured his mother's barrenness. He chose the name Hastings later, after a missionary he admired.

His first education was at a Church of Scotland mission, but he left at a young age to run away to South Africa. Malawian legend has it that he walked the 1,000 miles, but took two years because he stopped to work as a hospital orderly and a water-pumper in a mine.

After eight years as a clerk at a Johannesburg gold mine, studying at night, he won help from a Methodist bishop to come to the United States. He studied at the Wilberforce Institute in Xenia, Ohio, and at Indiana University before becoming the only black to graduate from the University of Chicago in 1931.

He received an M.D. from Meharry Medical College in Nashville, then moved to Britain to train at the Universities of Glasgow and Edinburgh and study tropical medicine in Liverpool.

He prospered as a physician in suburban London, but in 1953, furious that Britain had allowed the establishment of the Federation of Rhodesia and Nyasaland instead of taking power away from white expatriates, he moved to the Gold Coast, now Ghana, and railed against British treachery. Despite their fear of his firebrand tendencies, the colonial authorities let him return in 1958 to lead the Nyasaland African Congress.

He had apparently forgotten his native tongue, but got an uproarious welcome when he told his audience in

English, borrowing from Patrick Henry, 'In Nyasaland, we mean to be masters. And if that is treason, make the most of it.'

Riots broke out, and he spent a year in prison in Rhodesia before being released to lead his new Malawi Congress party to victory in a 1961 election. He told white settlers to accept majority rule 'or pack up.'

Sixty-five years of British rule ended in 1964 and the Federation dissolved in 1963, and he became Prime Minister of a nation that adopted a red, black and green flag with a rising sun as its symbol.

He took the presidency when Malawi became a Republic in 1966. Over the years, his rule became more idiosyncratic and more vicious. Former allies died in jail and rioters died in the streets.

Toward the end, he suffered from senility, had brain surgery in 1993 and seemed very dependent on Miss Kadzamira and her uncle, John Tembo, the Minister of State.

In 1994, under pressure from Western nations who cut off aid to enforce demands for democratic reforms, he called elections. He was defeated by Bakili Muluzi, a former protégé who had resigned from the Cabinet in 1982 suspecting he was about to be killed. His replacement, Mr. Muluzi said, was murdered.

After Dr. Banda was removed, he was tried for the 1983 murder of three Cabinet minsters and a Member of Parliament who were beaten to death with crowbars and hammers by the police and stuffed into a blue Peugot that was then pushed over a cliff in a staged accident. He was excused from court because of sickness, and ultimately was acquitted.

The Malawi Government said today that Dr. Banda would be given a state funeral on Dec. 3 with a 19-gun salute and military honors. He is to lie in state at New State House in Lilongwe beginning on Friday."

And he kept his country isolated from the rest of Africa except apartheid South Africa and other white-ruled territories in the region – Rhodesia and Mozambique – with whom he maintained close ties in defiance of the wishes of other independent countries on the continent.

But today, Malawi serves as vital link between East Africa and Southern Africa. And it has excellent relations with a country – Tanzania – with whom it was at odds during the liberation struggle in southern Africa. Tanzania was the headquarters of the liberation movements in Africa and strongly supported the freedom fighters in southern Africa while Malawi, under Banda, did not.

Malawi is divided into three administrative regions: Northern, Central and Southern.

The capital of Malawi is Lilongwe. It is roughly located in the centre of the country and is the largest city.

Blantyre is the second-largest. It is also the nation's commercial centre and is named after the birthplace in Scotland of the first European to discover Lake Nyasa, the English explorer Dr. David Livingstone.

The Great Rift Valley runs through the country from north to south. To the east of the valley lies Lake Nyasa, also known as Lake Malawi to Malawians. In neighbouring Tanzania, it is always called Lake Nyasa, *not* Lake Malawi.

The lake makes up about three-quarters of Malawi's eastern boundary. Lake Nyasa is 365 miles long and 52 miles wide. It is sometimes called the Calendar Lake because of those numbers which match the annual calendar.

There is one main river in Malawi: The Shire. It flows from the south end of Lake Nyasa and joins the Zambezi River farther south in Mozambique.

The Zambezi, also spelled as Zambesi, is one of the largest and longest rivers in Africa; it is the fourth-longest. And it is the largest flowing into the Indian Ocean.

Twenty per cent of Malawi's landmass consists of

water.

The topography varies extensively. There is the high Nyika plateau in the north and the Shire River valley in the south. The valley is a part of the Great Rift Valley which runs all the way from Lebanon to Mozambique.

In the far southeastern part of the country is Mount Mulanje. It is the highest mountain in Malawi and one of the highest in Africa.

Malawi has a hot climate in the low-lying areas in the south and a temperate climate in the northern highlands.

The Shire Highlands located east of the Shire River in the southern part of Malawi is a major agricultural area. It is also the most densely-populated part of the country.

Malawi is one of the least developed countries in the world and even in Africa itself. Most of the people live in the rural areas. And its economy is based on agriculture. The country has few minerals.

Agriculture accounts for more than 90 per cent of Malawi's export earnings, contributes 45 per cent of the gross domestic product (GDP), and supports 90 per cent of the population.

Malawi has some of the most fertile land in the region. Almost 70 percent of the country's agricultural produce comes from small-holder farmers.

The main crops are tobacco, tea, sugarcane, cotton, maize, sweet potatoes, groundnuts and sorghum.

Livestock, especially cattle and goats, are also an important part of the economy.

The main industries are tobacco, coffee, tea and sugar processing, sawmill products, cement and a variety of consumer goods, mainly import-substitution items.

Tobacco is the main foreign-exchange earner. It accounts for about 70 per cent of export revenues. But such heavy dependence on tobacco places a heavy burden on the economy as world prices decline and the international community increases pressure to limit tobacco production.

The country also relies heavily on tea, sugar and coffee. Together with tobacco, they constitute more than 90 per cent of Malawi's export revenue.

Other exports include cotton, groundnuts, wood products and apparel.

The most common food in Malawi is *nsima*. It is a standard dish of boiled maize flour. It is a thick porridge eaten with beans, meat or vegetables.

Rice, potatoes and cassava are also common food items.

Fish are also an important part of the diet. There are plenty of fish in Lake Nyasa. Others are caught in rivers and small lakes.

Fruits also are plentiful in Malawi. They include mangoes, melons, oranges, bananas, and pineapples.

Also, millions of people in villages and even in towns have chickens. They eat chicken and also have an ample supply of eggs.

Because foods are not widely imported, the availability of agricultural products depends on the growing season.

Tomatoes, onions, bananas and a few varieties of greens are available year round.

Other fruits and vegetables such as pineapples, guavas, mangoes, papayas, tangerines, lemons, cucumbers, eggplants, carrots, green peppers, and cabbage are also available depending on the season and region.

Foods that can be stored easily – such as groundnuts, maize, and beans – can be purchased cheaply at harvest time but increase in price as the year progresses.

Some fresh food products are imported. They include grapes, strawberries, garlic, broccoli and cauliflower from South Africa and Zimbabwe. These are sold outside import shops in the cities. But the cost is high and most Malawians can't afford that.

The biggest market for Malawian products in Africa is South Africa, followed by Zimbabwe.

And the countries on the continent which are the major

source of products destined for Malawi are South Africa, Zambia and Tanzania.

But like all other countries on the continent, Malawi also exports its products to other countries outside Africa. And it imports goods from overseas.

The country had a population of about 18 million in 2016. But the AIDS pandemic has had a profound impact on population growth. And it remains a major problem as in many other countries in the region and elsewhere in Africa.

Although the vast majority of the people are black African, significant numbers of whites and people of Asian descent also live in Malawi. Whites are mostly British, and Asians mostly Indian and Pakistani. They live mostly in towns and cities unlike their black counterparts more than 80 per cent of whom live in villages in the rural areas throughout Malawi.

Black Malawians are members of extended families so common across Africa. A common feature of extended families is cooperation among family members and even with neighbours not related to them. Many Malawians live with their extended families in huts or houses which are grouped together to form villages.

Malawi has a number of ethnic groups or tribes. They are of Bantu origin.

They include the Chewa, Tumbuka, Yao, Ngoni, Tonga, Ngonde also known as Nyakyusa (I am a Nyakyusa myself), Lomwe, and Sena.

Others include the Ndali and the Lambya who also live in Tanzania like the Nyakyusa do. More than 1 million Nyakyusas live in Tanzania, and fewer than that, about 400,000, in Malawi. The three ethnic groups straddle the Tanzanian-Malawian border.

The Chewa are the largest ethnic group in Malawi. They live mostly in the central and southern parts of the country.

The Yao, who live around the southern area of Lake

Nyasa, are also a major tribe in southern Tanzania and in northern Mozambique.

English is the official language of Malawi. It is widely spoken especially in major towns. You can also find people who speak English even in remote rural areas.

The main African language spoken in Malawi is Chichewa. It is spoken by almost 60 per cent of the population.

The other major languages are Chinyanja, spoken by about 13 per cent, Chiyao spoken by more than 10 per cent, and Chitumbuka spoken by almost 10 per cent.

Another language spoken by a large number of people in Malawi is Ngonde-Nyakyusa. It's spoken by 400,000 in northern Malawi bordering Tanzania; followed by Lomwe spoken by 300,000 in the southeastern part of the country. Lomwe is also spoken in Mozambique. And there is a variation in the language resulting in two distinct varieties: Malawian Lomwe and Mozambican Lomwe.

Another language spoken by a significant number of people in Malawi is Kokola. It is spoken by about 200,000 people, also in the southeast like Lomwe.

Sena – Malawian Sena – is spoken by about 270,000 in southern Malawi.

Tonga is spoken by around 170,000 in the north.

Other languages include Ndali spoken by around 70,000 in the northwestern part of Malawi bordering Tanzania, and Lambya spoken by about 50,000 also in the northwest.

Most of the people in Malawi are Christian. At least 80 per cent of the population were Christian. The Roman Catholic Church and the Church of Central African Presbyterians – also known as CCAP – are the largest.

There are other Christian denominations. But they are much smaller than the Catholic Church and the Presbyterian Church of Central Africa. They include the Anglican, Baptist, Evangelical and Seventh-Day Adventist churches.

Jehovah Witnesses are also an integral part of life in Malawi. And they have had an impact on the country in terms of national image because of the mistreatment they suffered at the hands of the authorities during President Banda's autocratic rule. Their sect was outlawed by Banda's regime. However, Dr. Banda's successor, Bakili Muluzi, restored its legal status in 1995 and Jehovah Witnesses have thrived since then.

Christianity has had the biggest impact on Malawi more than any other religious faith unlike, for example, in neighbouring Tanzania where Islam has been equally competitive with Christianity claiming about the same number of adherents – roughly 35 per cent Moslem and 35 per cent Christian – with the remainder being followers of traditional religions and other faiths.

And like everywhere else in Africa, the impact of Christianity in Malawi has been both positive and negative.

Some of the biggest achievements by Christian missionaries include provision of education and medical services.

On the negative side has been erosion of traditional values, customs and traditions under the influence of Christianity which in many cases is synonymous with Western civilisation:

"Christianity has a huge presence in Malawi . Until 2001, Bible Knowledge was a required subject for all Malawian secondary school students – it has since been replaced with a Religious Education curriculum that includes other world religions.

Christianity was first introduced to Malawians by David Livingstone and other missionaries who worked along the lake shore in the late 1800's.

Christianity spread rapidly under British colonialism despite an initially hostile welcome.

Now most villages have a mission or an extension of

some Christian sect. Some of the missions provide vocational training, schools, or hospitals at low cost for the local community.

Services are in the local language in all areas and areas with large populations of whites/expatriates may offer services in English.

Although Christianity has had a number of positive influences on Malawi (i.e. education and provision of health care institutions), it has not been without cost.

In many cases Christianity considers traditional beliefs and ways of living to be incompatible or inferior, and as a result, these cultural values have dwindled, if not disappeared altogether.

Which is not to say that traditional beliefs do not have a place in contemporary Malawian spiritual life. Despite a strong mission presence in Malawi's history and society, the Christianity that Malawians practice does not completely conform to a Western model.

For many Malawians, Western Christian beliefs are intertwined with traditional African practices and beliefs. For example, it is not uncommon to find men who consider themselves Christians, but have multiple wives or mistresses.

In addition, many Malawian Christians consult traditional healers or even participate in the traditional beliefs of Gule Wamkulu. While these practices are not necessarily non-Christian, they are different from the traditional Anglo-Saxon variety of Christianity with which Americans are familiar.

The second most prominent religion in Malawi is Islam – Muslims make up 15-20% of the population.

Islam was introduced by Arab slave traders who traveled largely by boat. They reached Malawi via the lake in the early 1800's, and converted tribes along the lake shore.

The people of the Yao tribe along the southern lake shore are most strongly associated with Islam. Almost every village in the areas of Balaka, Machinga, and Mangochi has a mosque. Many women in these areas wear veils that cover their heads, but not their faces, and some boys learn Arabic and Kiswahili to pursue study of the Koran.

Conflict between Christians and Muslims is rare in Malawi ; when it does erupt, as occurred in mid-2003, it is usually politically motivated.

Political affiliation, religious persuasion, and tribal identity are closely bound together in Malawi, and mosques are one of the most visible elements of that identity.

Outside of election time, relations between Christianity and Islam are quite calm. Malawians are generally tolerant of the three Old Testament religions, and tend to be more concerned about whether or not a person actively worships a god than what form that worship takes.

Indigenous beliefs and religions make up approximately 5% of the population, though they are rarely discussed, especially in Christian circles. Nonetheless, their influence is profound: nearly every market has a section or two for the local African doctor's medicines, and Gule Wamkulu dancers are present at many funerals.

Gule is an animistic religion common among the Chewa tribe in the central region. In Gule Wamkulu, the 'big dance,' leading dancers are elaborately costumed in ragged cloths, animal skins and usually a mask, all of which are designed to project the spirit they embody while dancing.

The dancers themselves form a secret society that follows stringent initiation practices and meets in cemeteries – a practice which sets them apart from ordinary Chewa. Generally, cemeteries are taboo for any purpose other than a funeral." – (Friends of Malawi (FOM), "Religion in Malawi").

There is, of course, a significant Muslim population as noted above, but estimates vary. Some say about 13 per cent of Malawians are Muslim, mostly Sunni. The Yao constitute the largest number of Muslims among native Africans.

There are also Hindus, Jews, Baha'is, Rastafarians and others. A significant number of people, including Christian converts, are also adherents of traditional religious practices.

Traditional religious beliefs are deeply rooted in traditional African societies especially in the rural areas. And Malawi is no exception. It is an integral part of the African way of life and culture. That is why even many Christians have not entirely abandoned their traditional religious practices. Many of them still make offerings to departed ancestors. Some of the offerings include animal sacrifices, a common practice in many parts of Africa. Even some Christians do that.

Usually people who have been converted to Christianity won't admit they follow traditional beliefs. And many Africans who have been modernised – euphemism for westernised – or urbanised shun those practices.

But a significant number of them still practise traditional religious beliefs and make offerings to appease ancestral spirits and seek guidance from them. And there are such people in Malawi just like in other African countries.

There is also a major difference between the people in the rural areas and those who live in towns.

People in the rural areas are more conservative and have great respect for traditional values and customs deeply rooted in African culture than their urbanised counterparts do.

Among many urban dwellers, there has been an erosion of African culture – values and customs – threatening to weaken or undermine their identity as Africans; a problem compounded by propagation of alien ideas and values.

Many Africans in urban areas are mesmerised by Western civilisation which has had a profound impact on the people of Malawi and others across Africa since colonial times even in some parts of the rural areas. They think foreign influence, especially Western, is better than their African traditional way of life.

But in spite of all that, African culture is still strong in Malawi.

One of the most important aspects of Malawian culture is traditional music and dances. Marriage ceremonies and initiation rites are some of the social and religious activities accompanied by traditional music and dances in different parts of Malawi.

In fact, music from Malawi has had a big impact beyond its borders on countries such as Zimbabwe and South Africa which have drawn a large number of immigrants from that country through the years. This has been going on for decades since colonial times when many people from Nyasaland – now Malawi – went to work in the mines in Southern Rhodesia (Zimbabwe) and in South Africa.

One of the best and most well-known kinds of music which originated from Nyasaland in Kwela. It became extremely popular in South Africa where it assumed the status of "national" music. And it is now claimed as South African music and a product of South Africa, although it actually originated in Nyasaland.

One of the most popular kwela musicians was South African pennywhistler Spokes Mashiyane. He was an embodiment of kwela together with other prominent and highly influential artists such as Lemmy Special Mabaso, simply known as Lemmy Special, another South African.

Efforts are also being made to preserve and promote traditional music in Malawi. According to a report on BBC Africa by Nikki Jecks entitled "Reviving Malawi's Music Heritage," 6 August 2009:

"You might not think you know much about Malawian music, but chances are you have heard it, or at least musicians influenced by it.

African music in general first came to international attention in the 1950s with the popularity of 'kwela' in the urban townships of Johannesburg.

South Africa claims kwela for its own, but Kenny Gilmore, the director of a documentary that charts the history of Malawian music, says kwela was actually popularised in South Africa by Malawian musicians.

'The founding fathers of kwela kwela, a lot, not all of them, were Malawian, Malawi's never been that famous so nobody hears about them,' he told the BBC World Service.

'Then they take a holiday down to South Africa, play some music, then, boom, the kwela kwela revolution [happens] and everybody thinks it's South African.'

Even a capella made famous by groups like Ladysmith Black Mambazo, and more contemporary styles like Afro-jazz, both owe much of their distinct style to Malawian musicians according to Mr Gilmore.

Melting pot

Malawi has nine tribal and linguistic groups, each possessing its own traditional dances and indigenous rhythms.

'True African music all comes from a traditional dance somewhere...and Malawi has got unique dances with unique rhythms,' he says.

He cites dances such as the Chewa's masked 'Gule Wamkulu' (the big dance); the Ngoni's 'Ingoma' war dance; the Beni military dance; and the healing 'Vimbuza' spirit dance of the Tumbuka.

But sadly only a handful of these were recorded in the 1940s and 1950s.

Inspired by the late musical archivist Alan Lomax's

famous journey to collect early blues recordings in the deep American South, for six weeks last year Mr Gilmore and his team travelled to villages across Malawi hoping to document and record some of this musical heritage, both past and present.

He hoped to record as much as possible of what is left of these traditions before the memories and the music are gone forever.

'Outside Malawi you never hear the words 'music' and 'Malawi' next to each other. I went to Cape Town record shops, nothing, London, nothing, America, New York, nothing.

'I'm on a mission to change it, I think the world needs to hear music and Malawi in the same sentence.'

Using a portable studio, musicians from Malawi's most rural and remote areas were given the opportunity to record, promote and preserve their musical heritage.

What the team got was a mix of individual musicians, small groups and cultural dance troupes, some of it purely traditional, some of it more of a fusion of traditional with contemporary and jazz influences.

'Sometimes you get these places in the world when you get these really interesting melting pots of cultures,' says Mr Gilmore.

'You have the Congolese influence just above Malawi, you've got the Zambian influence to the west, you've got Zimbabwe to the east and you've got South Africa to the south.

'These country boundaries actually mean nothing in cultural terms – so all these great influences come into Malawi, mixing – we've got a unique musical melting pot.'

'Massive riotous party'

Well-known Malawian musician and politician Lucius Banda says what makes Malawi music so special and deserving of greater interest is the way it has absorbed other influences into its musical traditions, making them their own.

'Malawi music is different, the special thing about Malawi music is [that it is] so cultural,' he says

'South Africa has disco and other Western influences. But Malawian music is quite unique in its own perspective.'

One such influence which dramatically influenced the country's musical style was the banjo.

The banjo was brought back to Malawi by soldiers who had served in East and Western African battalions during WWII.

The banjo and blue grass influences were infused with traditional beats and dominated the country's music for nearly 20 years.

In the 1970s jazz made an appearance in Malawi, then in more recent times has come gospel, reggae and pop influences.

But what is most special about Malawi music according to Mr Gilmore is not the way it has fused the traditional with the contemporary – it is its energy and passion.

'I've played around the world and most of the times you get the beginning and it's warming up, people not getting too excited, then there's a kind of warm phase.

'In Malawi, from the first song boom, the whole club just kind of ignites in a fire bomb and it carries on until the last.

'The bartenders have left the bar, security have left the gate, someone's climbed over the fence you can see the whole nearby village dancing next to the gate.

'It's just a massive riotous party and it just leaves me filled with so much happiness.'"

The same report was also published in a Malawian newspaper, *The Daily Times*, 12 August 2009.

The people of Malawi are also known for making

baskets and carvings some of which have won international acclaim. These products are very popular with tourists. They are also popular in urban areas where they are sold to foreigners and other people including Malawians themselves.

Through the years especially since independence, the people of Malawi have achieved a remarkable degree of unity transcending tribal loyalties and differences, although they have not been as successful as their counterparts in neighbouring Tanzania where tribalism has never been a major problem. But Malawians are more united than many other people in a number of countries on the continent.

Yet, in spite of all that success, regional loyalties remain strong in Malawi in some cases; for example, during national elections when politicians and their supporters exploit regional differences and capitalise on ethno-regional loyalties.

Major political parties are somewhat aligned along regional lines. Most of the Chewa identify with the Malawi Congress Party (MCP) which ruled Malawi for about 30 years under the leadership of President Hastings Kamuzu Banda, the most prominent Chewa in the country's post-colonial history.

The United Democratic Front is strong among the Yao and other groups in the Southern Region. It also produced a president, Bakili Muluzi, a Yao and a Muslim, who succeeded Banda in 1994 after winning the first multi-party elections in Malawi's history since independence.

Tribalism also remains a problem but not of the virulent kind as in Nigeria, Kenya, Rwanda and Burundi where ethnic rivalries have led to bloodshed through the years. In fact, it almost destroyed Kenya in 2007 after the general election which was conducted along ethno-regional lines. That is unthinkable in Malawi. There has never been such bloodshed.

The people

THE people of Malawi are known for their hospitality. Many people who visit Malawi return to their home countries with fond memories of the people they met in this country. Malawi is also known as "the warm heart of Africa" because of the warmth and friendliness of the people.

Chewa

The Chewa, who constitute the largest ethnic group in Malawi, are closely related to the people who live around them. These are mostly the Tumbuka and the Nsenga.

The Chewa are also historically related to the Bemba of Zambia. The Bemba are the largest ethnic group in Zambia. And like all the Bantu groups in East, Central and Southern Africa, they all trace their origin to what is now the Democratic of Congo (DRC) and, before then, West Africa especially in Cameroon and the eastern part of Nigeria.

The Chewa are also sometimes known as Nyanja. But many of them don't like the term because the word *nyanja* means "lake" – in Nyakyusa language which I also speak *nyanja* or *inyanja* also means "lake" – and refers to the broader range of peoples who also speak Chewa as a first or second language. They are called Nyanja.

And because Chewa is the common language in the

Lake Malawi area, it is often called Nyanja, a term derived from *Chinyanja* which means "Language of the Lake."

Many smaller tribes like the Ngoni, who traditionally speak a Nguni language related to Zulu, now speak Chewa/Nyanja as their mother tongue or first language.

The Chewa are divided into two subgroups or clans: the Phiri and the Banda. These are also some of the most well-known names for individuals in Malawi, including some of the nation's most prominent leaders through the years.

Chewa society is matrilineal. The language is called Chichewa. It is related to Shona, the main language spoken in Zimbabwe. This linguistic affinity points to a common origin in the Congo.

Like the Chewa and the Bemba, the Shona also migrated from what is today the Democratic Republic of Congo. The Bemba settled in what is Zambia today; the Shona moved farther south to Zimbabwe, and the Chewa went southeast, settling in what came to be known as Malawi.

The first president of Malawi, Dr. Hastings Kamuzu Banda, was a Chewa. It was also during his reign that Chichewa became the national language of Malawi. But English is still the official language as it has always been since colonial times. However, it was not until 1968 – about two years after independence – that Chewa and English were made the official languages of Malawi.

And, coincidentally, the capital of Malawi – Lilongwe – is also located in the homeland of the Chewa in the Central Region.

As the largest ethnic group, the Chewa are scattered throughout the country. But the vast majority of them still live in the Central Region.

The Chewa also live in Zambia. They are a part of one of the larger ethno-linguistic groups in that country known as Nyanja-Chewa.

And since they are representative of Malawi in some

fundamental respects as the largest ethnic group and as the custodians of the "national language" because it is their indigenous language, it is important to take a comprehensive look at them; not only because of their status in Malawi but also on the continent as one of Africa's most prominent groups:

"The Chewa are predominantly concentrated within the central region, surrounding the capital city of Lilongwe, in areas such as Dedza, Kasungu, Dowa, Ntchisi, Mchinjui, Ntcheu, Salima, and Nkhota Kota....

Although English has been the official language in Malawi since 1968, Chichewa has remained the national language, meaning present day Malawian culture includes significant Chewa influence.

For the Chewa, this is empowering – meaning education systems, health care, publications, governing boards, and radio broadcasts all utilize Chichewa, opening a wide opportunity of exposure to an outside world....

Man-made borders are useless to people whose culture originates from descendants of a different type of unity. Perhaps Chewa now consider their identity as Malawian and Bantu, or perhaps they have simply learned to fulfill the duties of a number of identities in order to better their own livelihood.

Although Malawians demonstrate comparatively strong national unity, the Chewa have not lost their tribal unifications and divisions.

Within the Chewa there exist various clans; cousins if you will. The Banda and Phiri clans, for example, represent some of the largest groups, evident through the popularity of this clan name as a surname.

Traditionally, stories also hold that the Chewa themselves came from a merger of the Banda and Phiri clans....

Chewa Traditions

The Chewa believe that living things were created by God – Chiuta – on the mountain of Kapirintiwa, which borders present-day Malawi and Mozambique.

Ancestors and spirits of other living creatures play an important part in present-day society by being in constant contact with the living world, predominately (sic) through dance of those initiated to *Nyau*, or secret societies.

'Gule Wamkulu,' literally meaning 'big dance,' has become a sort of title for secret societies of traditional Chewa religious practices.

The Gule Wamkulu ceremonies consist of formally organized dances to admire the remarkable physical abilities of these individuals – considered to be adept at their dance as a result of their spiritual state.

Informally, Gule Wamkulu, or 'Gule,' is a term associated with anyone who participates in the rituals of these secret societies.

The peak season for Gule occurs in July, with young men dressed as ancestral animals, trees, or in masks of ancestral spirits.

The Gule themselves are initiated through formal ceremony into this society.

Gule are considered to be in 'animal state' when they are dressed in such attire, and are not to be approached.

If one has the misfortune of passing a Gule on the road, traditional behavior consists of dropping a few coins for the Gule – never handing them the money directly for fear they will grab you and take you to the cemetery for ritual purposes.

Generally, it is best to avoid Gule in informal situations. In their animal or ancestral state, they are unpredictable.

Within the village, Gule may appear in small groups of 4 or 5 and villagers do their best to avoid any encounters.

Gule are common in the afternoons, a strong incentive for tending to all business outside the home in the early hours.

These secret societies have allowed for a close knit kinship between members of the Chewa – and equally divided them from neighbor(ing) groups.

In a village known for its abundance of Gule's, I once made the mistake of making my way back home in the late afternoon. As the Gule's ran through the village, I ran too – into the opening door of a stranger.

A local village woman who did not know me flung open her door offering her home as a sanctuary. Together we watched – unable to speak each other's language – as the Gule ran past her window. I understood that it is not only the Gule Wamkulu themselves who receive the feeling of community, and solidarity, but also they who provide such to the rest of us.

The following day I planned to leave the village, but villagers suggested I wait a few more days until the festivities of Gule's had passed. By doing so, it was anticipated that during my two-mile journey to the main road I would encounter fewer Gule's.

In my urgency to leave, I summoned the help of a middle-aged man who had an 'exemption' from Gule harm. The man was lucky enough to own a bicycle and he traveled quite frequently to town. Because he was at risk for increased interaction with Gule, he had requested to witness the Gule ceremonies.

After paying a small sum of money, he had become a sort of honorary Gule, to whom no harm would come. He had 'bought the way.'

But he still would not accompany me on my journey to the main road.

'I will take you in two days; I don't want money to take you now...wait two days and we will go.'

Take me in two days he did – and our trip was Gule free!

Formally, the Gule Wamkulu dance is performed when the headman requests such festivities, generally corresponding with weddings, funerals, or initiation rite ceremonies.

The dances are a great source of celebration, and although the mystery and excitement still surrounds the presence of the Gule Wamkulu, the community reacts to their show with great giddiness and giggles.

There are a number of traditional dances of the Gule Wamkulu, all performed for various events.

The 'Zilombo,' or masked dancers, perform with extraordinary movements and energy, wearing elaborate traditional masks and attire.

According to local folklore, it is said that the Queen of England witnessed a traditional Gule Wamkulu celebration, and was so captivated she asked to take some home; a request that was unfulfilled.

Masks worn by the Gule Wamkulu include thousands of different representations – generally each developed hundreds of years ago by unique tribes, and accented with their own individual touch – for example one accenting bright colors, one dark.

Today, these masks, with their different origins, are part of what is now the Chewa culture.

The female version of Gule Wamkulu, called Chisamba, occurs for female initiation rituals. During this ceremony a woman is taken into a private room, and instructed by her elders on how to be a proper woman.

The solidarity of these women does not diminish after the ceremony, but rather is rooted during this event. The celebratory Chisamba dance accompanies this event. Historically, a number of initiation practices have been involved – today these words of wisdom and celebratory event comprise the event.

The presence of Christian missionaries has resulted in large numbers of converts throughout Malawi – although this was not always the case.

In the 19th century, converts to Christianity from all tribes were often asked to cut all ties with other Chewa.

It is believed that Christianity among the Chewa has increased in part because of the Dutch missionary influence since the mid 1980's.

However, the Gule Wamkulu, the Chewa language, and the Chewa traditions appear deep-rooted among these people, and changing their spiritual beliefs doesn't appear to have taken away their traditional ceremony – maybe it's only taken away those willing to do so publicly.

Chewa Village Life

Within a Chewa village the chiefs are a central unit of rule.

Village life is somewhat self-contained, although not independent.

Typical homes have numerous commodities that are purchased or obtained through bartering.

Lamps, chairs, oil, salt, mats for sitting, pots and pans, and jewelry are commonly seen within the homes of some villagers.

Chewa communities cover a vast land area and individual communities have progressed at their own pace. Those near the main road, for example, have increasingly adjusted to outside influence while those closer to the lake have developed a dependency and connection to utilization of this body of water.

Chewa rural life revolves around agricultural activities geared towards increasing production of maize (corn), vegetables, and groundnuts. All of these crops are used for consumption, and any excess is sold either within the village or occasionally at the increasing markets scattered along the roadside.

The only crop produced predominately (sic) for sale in Chewa villages in central Malawi is tobacco.

Tobacco is started slightly before maize, however the

two crops are produced during the same season. This time of year, during land preparation, planting and maintaining crops, and of course the tremendously important harvest, provide focal points for the year.

Because of the physical structure of the village, most farmland is located on the outskirts of the village, often requiring long walks to and from the fields. Because of this, there are generally small gardens, known as *dimba*, located nearby the home where vegetables and small amounts of maize are grown. If any of these crops are sold, the income usually belongs to the woman of the house.

Land ownership is determined by the village headman, and is constantly changing.

With births, marriages, and deaths come changes in one's land allotment. Sometimes a husband and wife will have their own land, while sometimes they will share, in which case the husband decides if and how to sell the excess.

Traditionally, the Chewa were described as a matrilineal society, however the Chewa today include influences of both matrilineal and patrilineal leadership.

Landowners are considered to be of higher status, however owning more land means working more land, and this often requires hiring additional labor. This informal employment consists of hiring neighbors to work as 'Ganyu' or informal laborers.

Women and men are hired as Ganyu labor, and payment is usually made in maize itself, and is often given upon completion of a particular project. Ganyu labor is essential to the functioning of the village, and creates a strong interdependency on one another.

Children are also a valuable source of labor, with young boys beginning to assist in farm activities around the age of six or seven.

Young girls are also valuable to the functioning of these activities, as they are responsible for the laborious chores of fetching water, caring for younger children, helping their mothers cook, clean, take maize to the mill, and look after the sick.

In addition, women and children laboriously process the staple crop of maize into the commonly eaten 'Nsima.' Nsima requires much preparation; first the maize is dried, sorted, pounded, and finally cooked into a pasty patty. Routinely prepared with whatever vegetables are available, Nsima is eaten with the hands and used as a palate with which to scoop up the rest of the meal.

Since planting generally occurs around November, with the harvest seen near June, the days in between are filled with laborious work for adults and children.

From June to October, however, the days are sometimes long and filled with much more free time.

All households are required to spend a certain amount of time participating in activities that enhance village life – sometimes construction of the church, work on an elderly person's land, or simply assisting as instructed by the village headman.

In today's modern-day Chewa villages, the option exists to replace the community service hours with a simple payment to the village headman, intended as a contribution towards the community project.

Aside from community service, some village women will engage in additional income-generating activities, such as the sale of small goods (usually from the house garden), or occasionally crafted or handmade goods.

Men sometimes will seek outside employment, perhaps working for daily salary in the nearby tea plantations of central Malawi, or involve in making and selling bricks, which are burned in ovens....

Often times, however, these months are filled with hardship. Households struggle to make sure their maize supply will last through these months, and to avoid the downfall of disease.

Formal village events generally include typical

celebratory and mourning activities – birthdays, weddings, ritual transitions into adulthood, and the ever increasing funerals.

All celebrations are elaborate, and it is at these events that the spirit of traditional Chewa culture comes to life – that is, the spirits of Chewa ancestors, and revered animals – come to life." – (Amy Gough, "The Chewa," The Peoples of The World Foundation, 2004).

There are other well-known ethnic groups in Malawi. Even those not well-known outside Malawi are equally important.

But I have decided to focus on the Chewa because as the largest ethnic group in the country, and because of its influence across the nation in many areas – an influence facilitated by the status of the Chewa language as the national language – it is broadly representative of Malawi across the spectrum, especially as a microcosm of the nation's demographic composition.

The Chewa also share ethno-cultural, linguistic and historical ties with other groups, reinforcing their common identity as "one people" even before the coming of Europeans – who created African countries which exist today – and as Malawians in terms of national identity which also binds them as a collective entity.

Yao

The Yao, also known as Yawo, are the second-largest ethnic group in Malawi. They live mostly in the southern and southeastern parts of Lake Nyasa in Malawi and straddle the Malawian-Mozambican border.

They are found mostly in the following districts in the Southern Region: Mangochi, Chiradzulu, Zomba, Mulanje and Blantyre.

The migrated from Niassa province, in northwestern Mozambique, to the eastern part of Malawi in the 1830s.

They are also one of the largest ethnic groups in Tanzania. They live mostly in southern Tanzania and northern Mozambique – their original homeland – and straddle the Tanzanian-Mozambican border.

They constitute a single ethno-cultural entity across national boundaries constituting a cohesive entity across three countries although they are also divided within, having separate identities based on their national identities and religious beliefs and chiefdoms.

They are mostly farmers like other Malawians. But almost all of them are also Muslim, unlike most of their fellow countrymen – and women – who are mostly Christian. Their involvement with Arabs in trade including the slave trade is one of the the main reasons they converted to Islam. The Islamic faith was also compatible with their traditional way of life, both sanctioning polygamy. Other native practices and beliefs were also compatible with Islam in many respects.

About 99 per cent of the Yao are Muslim and only 1 per cent Christian. They are mostly subsistence and fishermen farmers like other Malawians and their pattern of life is basically traditional but with very strong Islamic influence. As farmers, they are known for their slash-and-burn techniques.

"Common crops include maize, beans, cassava, bananas, groundnuts (peanuts) and tobacco. The staple food is ugali, a stiff porridge made from maize flour and water. Ugali is most commonly formed into large patties and served with vegetables, meat, beans, or fish.

The Yawo are a matrilineal and largely matrilocal society. Family leadership roles are passed down through the female's family and upon marriage, a husband moves to his wife's village, where he remains somewhat of an outsider. Divorce rates are high and polygamy is common.

The Yawo speak Ciyawo, a Bantu language. Many Yawo also speak Cichewa, Malawi's nationalized trade

47

language. Malawi's Yawo have a low literacy rate compared to that of other ethnic groups in the country.

Respect and politeness are highly regarded among the Yawo and are taught to each generation during the initiation process. Greetings are important, with many children kneeling out of respect when greeting adults. In Yawo culture, it is the host (not the visitor) who initiates greetings. Children attend government schools, which are free for primary education and Yawo children often attend madrassah (Muslim) schooling in the afternoons to learn Arabic.

The Yawo have their own system of traditional governance, sorting out problems in local village courts, although ultimately, the Malawian government holds political and legal authority.

After being introduced to Islam in the late 1800s by Swahili-Arab slave traders, the Yawo converted to Islam and many began practicing Islam and their traditional religion in parallel. Today, Yawo Muslims belong predominantly to one of two groups of Muslims, both of which are Sunni. One group is Sufi in belief and practice and are known as the Qadiriyya. This group combines Islam with traditional African religion, using traditional medicines and talismans for protection from sorcery and witchcraft, as well as for healing and obtaining good fortune. The other group is largely anti-Sufi and more scripturalist in their approach to Islam.

The Yawo are a resistant people group. They have insulated themselves from responding to Christian witness by maintaining their unified language, cultural and religious differences. Although their Chewa neighbors have been Christianized for many years (since David Livingstone and early missionaries entered Malawi), the Yawo have remained virtually unreached and have not responded to evangelism by the Chewa. In general, the Chewa have not reached out to the Yawo using Ciyawo or culturally appropriate methods.

Along with deep spiritual needs, the Yawo also suffer from physical needs. HIV/AIDS has been a serious problem in Malawi, though in recent years increased education, awareness and aid have proved profitable (statistically). Malaria and malnutrition are two other physical challenges the Yawo face." – ("The Yaw of Africa," joshuaproject.net).

Other Malawians in different parts of the country face the same problems only in varying degrees mainly because of poverty.

Their traditional way of life is centred on villages which constitute vital social units headed by headmen:

"The Yao live in compact villages of 75 to 100 persons under traditional headmen. These headmen, like the chiefs, succeed matrilineally, the office usually going to the eldest sister's firstborn son.

On marriage the man leaves his village to live in that of his wife, so that villages are composed basically of groups of women related through the female line, together with their spouses.

Yao social life features annual initiation ceremonies involving circumcision for boys. Originally, these ceremonies were closely connected with the worship of ancestor spirits, but through Arab contact most Yao are Muslims, and the rites incorporate Islamic elements." – ("Yao: An African People," *Encyclopaedia Britannica*).

Economically, they are some of the most successful people in Malawi; an achievement partly if not largely attributed to their long involvement in commercial activities since they started trading with the Arabs and other coastal people before the colonisation of the area that came to be known as Nyasaland, now Malawi.

Lomwe

The Lomwe are the third-largest ethnic group in Malawi after the Chewa and one of the four largest in the country.

They live mostly in Phalombe District in the southeastern part of the country in the Southern Region. They are also found in smaller numbers throughout the province which is also home to Blantyre. The province had more than 6 million people in 2017.

Other districts which have significant numbers of the Lomwe are Mulanje, Thyolo, Chiradzulu, Zomba, and Liwonde, all in the Southern Region.

They straddle the Malawian-Mozambican border and are found in even larger numbers in Mozambique where they live mostly in Zambezi Province, their original homeland:

"The Lomwe are originally from what is now Mozambique to the east of Malawi. In 1996, a source indicated that the majority lived in Malawi. However, current sources now indicate that the population in Mozambique is about double that in Malawi. The total popualtion reported in current sources sources is also considerably less that the population reported in 1996.

In 1996 the figure reported by certain sources within Malawi was 1.8 million in Malawi and 1.35 millon in Mozambique. Today, a larger population of Lomwe live in Mozambique, about 1.3 million compared to about 700,000 million currently living in Malawi. However, we are aware that population figures are often unreliable in these countries. The Bible Society of South Africa says: 'Nearly 2 million people in Mozambique are Lomwe-speaking.'

The Ethnologue reported in 1996 that the total number

of Lomwe speakers (then considered one language in both countries) was 2,850,000. The Ethnologue reported new research in 2005, yielding a population of 1.3 million speakers of Lomwe (ngl) in Mozambique and only 250,000 speakers of Lomwe, Malawi (lon). Other sources report about 700,000 Lomwe in Malawi.

This figure of 700,000 may be the total ethnic figure in Malawi, since the Ethnologue reports that Chewa (Nyanja) is a mother tongue among many of the ethnic Lomwe in Malawi. The whole tribe seems to be shifting into the Chewa language stream, as are other small tribes in Malawi.

The migration of large numbers of Lomwe to Malawi had taken place before the arrival of missionaries, white traders, and colonialists in the latter part of the nineteenth century. There was also a large influx of Lomwe into Malawi in the 1930's because of tribal wars in Mozambique. A more recent contributor to the Lomwe migration to Malawi was Mozambique's long civil war. Perhaps many have now returned since the stablization of Mozambique.

The Lomwe are Bantu people as are most of the people of southeastern Africa. The Lomwe are part of a larger cluster called the Makhuwa-Lomwe Group. Together the tribes of this cluster make up almost 40% of the population of Mozambique. In the past Lomwe women made distinctive scarification marks on their cheeks, but this custom is dying out.

The Lomwe are a rural people with only 5-10% living in urban areas. They are primarily subsistence farmers. Many of them love to hunt though wild game is scarce.

The Lomwe language is written using the Roman alphabet. Lomwe people in Mozambique speak Elomwe as their heart language. In Malawi the situation is somewhat different. Although the Lomwe are continuing to keep many of their traditions, the Lomwe language is being used less and less with only the elderly still continuing to use it as their first language. In Malawi, most of the Lomwe speak Chichewa which was made one of the two national languages of Malawi in 1968.

Until recently linguists thought the sp;eech of all the Lomwe groups was one language. More recent research has shown tha Lomwe in Malawi is not mutually intelligible with Lomwe in Mozambique. The 2005 *Ethnologue* has reported them as two different languages. They call the Mozambique speech *Lomwe* and assign it the language code *ngl*. The speech of Malawi is called *Lomwe, Malawi* and has a code of *lon*.

Lomwe speakers are reported generally to have a low literacty rate. Exact literacy figures are vague.

Mozambique's muddy political history has not greatly influenced the rural dwelling Lomwe people, except to continue scattering the peoples over the area and into Malawi. Neither the Portuguese culture nor Marxist teaching were seriously embraced by these people. In Malawi, the three main parties are somewhat aligned along regional lines. The Lomwe identify mainly with the ruling party which is the predominant party in the Southern Region.

Lomwe customs are centered around work and play. The men build the houses, the barriers to protect the gardens, and the grain bins to store the maize. They also like to make grass or reed mats.

In the past the men have been skilled hunters, but there is little game remaining to be hunted. The major tasks of the women are cooking and caring for the children. Also they enjoy making clay pots. The young girls start helping their mothers at an early age often carrying their younger siblings on their backs when they can barely do so. The Lomwe enjoy working together as evidenced by friends and neighbors working together cultivating one another's fields.

The religious leaning of the Lomwe vary greatly with the degree of penetration of Christianity. The Baptist

Union in Mozambique has had a strong influence in areas surrounding its churches. However in general, the Lomwe are animists who still worship ancestral spirits. Though most Lomwe would consider themselves Christians, the traditions of the ancestors greatly influence their daily lives.

Recent analysis has led to a classification of religion for the Malawi Lomwe as Traditional Religion. In Mozambique, it is reported that Traditional Religion, Christianity and Islam are found among the Lomwe....

The Universities Mission to Central Africa began work at Magomero in Southern Malawi in 1861. As the Lomwe are one of three major ethnic groups in that area, they were among the first to receive a Christian witness in Malawi. So many of the Lomwe who came into Malawi from Mozambique in the 1930's were Roman Catholic that the Catholic Church in southeastern Malawi was sometimes called 'the Lomwe Church.'

Mozambique also has a greater than 100 year history of evangelistic effort among the Lomwe, especially due to the efforts of the Baptist Union of South Africa." – ("The Lomwe of Mozambique and Malawi," strategyleader.org/profiles/lomwe.html).

Although the Lomwe are the third-largest ethnic group in Malawi and constitute a vital component of the nation's identity, there are other groups which have historically been identified with the identity of Malawi as a nation, although smaller ones are no less important as equal members of society and as fellow Malawians. There are at least ten such groups whose identity is virtually synonymous with the national identity of Malawi.

Besides the Chewa, the Yao, and the Lomwe, the other major ones are the Nyanja, Tumbuka, Sena, Tonga, Ngoni, Ngonde and the Lambya/Nyiha.

Other main indigenous languages of Malawi besides

Chewa are Yao, Lomwe, and Tumbuka.

The dominance of Chewa as the main native language has also been impacted by the promotion of other local languages as a result of government policy to enhance their status.

Chewa was the only native *national* language from 1968 to 1994. After elevating other local languages to "national status," Chewa is now only one of the many native languages used in schools and in the media, although it has not completely lost its status as the main indigenous language of Malawi because of its dominance for many years. But it has lost its official status as the only official indigenous language.

The government officially decided in 1996 to provide education in native languages from Standard One to Standard Four, and in English from Standard Five because of its dominance in higher education. It is still the main language used in government, institutions of higher learning – colleges and universities – and in the judicial system and administration as well as in other areas of national life.

The widespread use of English in Malawi, as in other former British colonies across the continent, is probably the most enduring legacy of colonial rule in Africa, reinforced by its status as the main international language, eclipsing French, the second most widely used in the global arena.

Other ethnic groups

The Ngoni are the fourth-largest ethnic group in Malawi. They are also one of the major ethnic groups in Mozambique, Tanzania and Zambia.

The Tumbuka are the fifth-largest ethnic group in Malawi. Then there are the Sena, the Tonga, and the Ngonde.

Together with the Chewa, Yao and Lomwe, these groups constitute about 96 per cent of Malawi's population. The remainder are members of smaller ethnic groups including non-black minorities, mainly whites – British and others – and Asians, especially of Indian origin.

Ngoni

The Ngoni are some of the most well-known people in eastern and southern Africa. They are related to the Zulu. They left South Africa in the 1830s and settled in what is now Malawi, Zambia, Tanzania and Mozambique after a long trek north. They fled from their traditional homeland because of conflicts in Natal Province in the eastern part of the country following the emergence of the Zulu under the leadership of Shaka as the most powerful people in the region.

The dominance of the Zulu led to conflict with other groups, disrupting social life and ethnic alliances which had existed before.

The fame of the Ngoni in eastern Africa has to do with their reputation as fierce fighters probably more than anything else. They conquered different tribes as they moved north and incorporated them into their tribe. They were so successful in doing so that members of many tribes claimed they were Ngoni even when they were not. They did so out of fear and simply to claim the identity of a tribe they considered to be superior to them.

Their identity as an ethnic group is also questionable. As they moved north from South Africa and conquered other tribes, they became virtually a minority, outnumbered by the people they conquered. The majority of the people who claim to be Ngoni are a product of this mixture of different ethnic groups, with "pure" Ngonis being a very small minority. Yet, as a group, they retained many cultural aspects of the Zulu, especially in terms of military and social organisation but which were later superseded by the hybrid cultures from different tribes which were integrated into and absorbed by the Ngoni "tribe."

In Malawi, the Ngoni live mostly in the northern part of the country, especially in Mzimba District, and in the Central Region.

Mzimba District is also home to the Tumbuka and the main language spoken there is Tumbuka. But traditional rulers have always been Ngoni since it is a Ngoni stronghold and has been that way from the time the Ngoni conquered the area and absorbed members of the local tribes, mainly the Tumbuka.

The Ngoni also live in Ntcheu District in the Central Region. They are the largest ethnic group in the district and are descended from the Swazi of Swaziland and the Zulu of South Africa. They also have strong ties to their fellow Ngonis in neighbouring Mzimba District in the Northern Region.

They are also found in large numbers in Dowa District in the Central Region. They are the second-largest ethnic group in the district after the Chewa; the Yao the third-largest.

The Ngoni also live in significant numbers in Dedza District and in Mchnji District once known as Fort Manning District. Both districts are in the Central Region in west-central Malawi.

The identity of the Ngoni as an ethnic group was also a subject addressed by renowned British anthropologist, Margaret Read, in her article, "Tradition and Prestige among the Ngoni," in the *Journal of the International African Institute*:

"Before I made my first camp in an Ngoni village, many Europeans had said to me, 'There are practically no Ngoni left to-day. They are all hopelessly mixed with other tribes. None of them keep to the Ngoni customs any longer. Their chiefs are no good.'

From the doorway of my hut I saw people coming all day long to the Paramount Chief, behaving towards him with profound respect, bringing him presents, working for him. His children formed a special group in the village, easily recognizable by their bearing and their manners. Old indunas came to instruct me, as they had instructed chiefs in their day, on the duties of a ruler, and the code of Ngoni laws. Old warriors in war dress came and danced by the cattle kraal and sang praise songs. Courts were held with scrupulous regard for order and justice. Other chiefs came visiting from distant parts with their retinues, and were received ceremonially.

It soon became apparent that here was the centre of a political state, whose head was invested with prestige and authority over a wide area, and where behaviour to the Paramount and to every one else was strictly regulated by custom, and as strictly observed. These were Ngoni, and they and their fellow Ngoni in other areas for the next ten months introduced me to the Ngoni people. The European assertion, that they no longer existed as a people, they laughed at, and proceeded to demonstrate that the contrary was true.

The Ngoni are found to-day scattered over four East African territories....The present divisions of the Ngoni are due partly to European frontiers, partly to the fact that more than one party of them came up from the south, and partly to divisions among the Ngoni during the period of settlement....

These groups of people with their southern origin, settled among people who had a totally different language and social structure, present to the anthropologist a highly complex situation to investigate. He must at the outset ask the questions, 'Who are these Ngoni? Have they a separate identity as a people, marked by distinctive social and political institutions ?'

After living among them for nearly a year I am convinced that it is correct to speak of the Ngoni as a distinctive group; that they themselves are very conscious of their separate identity as a people, and that they can point to certain of their institutions, notably their language and political, territorial, and kinship groupings, which are definitely Ngoni, that is, of southern origin, and which distinguish them from the people among whom they settled.

The complexities of this situation involve the analysing of the ethnic elements included in this term 'Ngoni' and the determining of the sense in which it is to be used. They involve also an explanation of what is meant by the expression 'a distinctive Ngoni culture,' or 'distinctive Ngoni institutions.'

The anthropologist who is interested in culture contact must go further and indicate the nature of the double contact caused first by the intermingling of the Ngoni with other tribes, and then by the advent of the Europeans. It is not possible in this article to do justice to all these aspects of an intricate problem. Stated very briefly, the problem is this: an Ngoni aristocratic minority created an Ngoni 'state' of mixed ethnic units, imposed a national identity on all who formed part of it, and inspired a real 'national feeling' among those who were assimilated." – (Margaret Read, "The Ngoni People of Africa: Tradition and Prestige among the Ngoni," *Journal of the International African Institute*, Vol. 9, No. 4, October 1936, Edinburgh University Press, pp. 453 – 484).

Therein lies the validity and legitimacy of the claim that the Ngoni do exist as a legitimate ethnic entity with its own distinct identity; not in the claim or the assertion that the Ngoni today, as a group or as a people, are all direct descendants of their ancestors who trekked north from Natal Province in South Africa. Some, if any; are; most are mixed with members of other tribes.

What gives them identity as Ngoni is their history, including their history as a product of mixed tribes, and their sense of common identity which is reinforced by the culture and traditions of the Ngoni conquerors from the south imposed on the people they conquered to create a unified whole that assumed a Ngoni identity. As Margaret Read stated:

"My thesis is that Ngoni 'national feeling' is based on the traditions of their past – on the story of their southern origin, their trek from the south, and their settlement in their present areas. I shall show how the continued preservation of their distinctive institutions, together with their strong historical sense, gave them a dominant position in the country, which was enforced through their military and political supremacy." – (Ibid.).

On how inclusive the term Ngoni is, and why even those who know they are not Ngoni in terms of ethnicity still identify themselves as Ngoni, Margaret Read explained this kind of identity in the following terms:

"In a number of the villages where no Ngoni clans were represented, the villagers nevertheless asserted, 'We are Ngoni, because we are the people of Mpezeni' (in Northern Rhodesia).
When questioned, they acknowledged their local origin as Nsenga or Chewa by kinship and clan, but claimed the name Ngoni in terms of their political allegiance.
It is worth while mentioning here that this claim to be Ngoni is made with even more force when men are away from home on the mines or at other work. I found men on the Northern Rhodesian Copper Belt and in Johannesburg assert emphatically that they were Ngoni because they were the people of Mpezeni or Gomani, at the same time giving their clan names with a grin because they knew it would reveal their Chewa or Nsenga origin.

It is 'the thing' to pass as Ngoni if you can carry it off and in strange places – where the acid test of the clan name is not known – it is easy to do this.

A group of Nyasaland men newly arrived on the Crown Mines in Johannesburg told me confidentially, 'Here we say only, 'We are all Ngoni.' You know that our clan names are Chewa or Tumbuka, but we are the people of Gomani or of Mwambera, and so we say we are Ngoni. And then people are respecting us.'

The prestige in the name Ngoni is a matter of pride, not only in their own country, but far and wide in Africa." – (Ibid.).

It important to emphasise that even Ngoni chiefs or other leaders of the Ngoni and influential members in the Ngoni community do know that they and all their people are not just "Ngoni." They are know they are a product of many tribes, and not just direct descendants of the original Ngoni who came from South Africa; a point underscored by Margaret Read:

"The chiefs and other important men among the Ngoni recognize that they are a very mixed group ethnically. When asked, 'What is the meaning of a clan ?' they reply, 'It shows a man's tribe that we may know how to respect him.'

It is hardly correct, therefore, to speak of the Ngoni as a tribe, for from Natal to Tanganyika men of many 'tribes' joined, or were captured and forcibly assimilated by, the original nucleus of Zulu and Swazi warriors, to be welded by their political and military organization into an effective group.

What meaning, therefore, can we give to the term 'Ngoni,' and how can this group which calls itself Ngoni be analysed into its component parts?" – (Ibid.).

She defined "Ngoni" in the following terms:

"The references made hitherto show that the term 'Ngoni' is used in several different connotations. It is, strictly speaking, an historical linguistic term, and referred originally to that group of clans described as 'Nguni' 'because they spoke a language classified today as the Nguni dialects.'

Somewhere on the march north the Ngoni changed the *u* to an *o*, and arrived in their present areas saying 'We are Ngoni.'

They assert emphatically that it was on the march they began to say 'We are Ngoni,' and they suggest that it was important to have some general term to cover individuals from many mixed groups.

The name Ngoni having been assumed on the march north, it obviously at first only covered those clans which were of true southern origin, or as we should say today, of Zulu or Swazi stock. This is the meaning which Ngoni still has when used in its narrow or strict sense today." – (Ibid.).

The Ngoni themselves acknowledge the nature of their ethnic identity as a product of many tribes. As Read stated in her article:

"In collecting the clan names in a village, for example, the headman says 'Those are Ngoni, those are Makalanga, those are Nsenga,' and so on.

The true Ngoni clans are those most highly honoured, the real aristocrats, and a little experience teaches the field worker to recognize their bearing as they walk about among the rest.

In a village containing several clans, the houses of the Ngoni clans occupy the most honourable places in the middle of the horse-shoe formation surrounding the cattle kraal. In any meeting at a chief's village the men and women of Ngoni clans sit nearest to the chief and drink beer before the rest.

This ranking by clans, however, does not stop at the true Ngoni. They lead the hierarchy, but other clans also claim precedence in a rough geographical order of the tribes absorbed from south to north. The true Ngoni illustrate this by saying, 'In old days the only men who were made indunas were those of the Swazi, Zulu, Suto, and Tonga clans. After we settled here, indunas were made from the Makalanga, Nsenga, and Sukuma clans.'

There is therefore a hierarchy of rank expressed in the clan names, and this rank is evident in the position of houses on a village site, and the degree of authority exercised by the clans and the respect' accorded to them.

In effect, all those whose ancestors were absorbed before the final break up of the main Ngoni group are recognized as having some claim to the name Ngoni. The rest, that is the clans found in the areas where the Ngoni finally settled are, or rather were, regarded as conquered or slave people." – (Ibid.).

She went on to state:

"We have seen, however, that there is a much wider sense in which the term Ngoni is used – that is, by all who live under the rule of the Paramount Chief. This extended usage is due to the prestige and honour in which the stricter meaning of Ngoni is held.

It was illustrated in the instance of the Nyasaland men in Johannesburg, who all claimed to be Ngoni because they had discovered at once that the name commanded respect among the mixture of tribes to be found on the mines.

Indunas and other leading men sometimes make use of this wider connotation when boasting about the large numbers of people owning allegiance to the Ngoni Paramount Chief, compared with the other petty chieftainships. 'All those in the country of Mpezeni are

Ngoni. All are his people.'

At the same time they make it clear that there is a distinction between the real Ngoni and the other subjects of the Paramount – a distinction which formerly was much sharper than it is today. All are the people of the Paramount, it is true, but in old days the majority of the non-Ngoni were called slaves.

To this day the Ngoni when angry may call out to someone, 'Chewa, Chewa,' implying ' Slave, slave', and be hauled to the chief's court for insulting language. There the chief will take pains to point out that there are no slaves today, and that no Ngoni must 'spoil the country' by insulting the people of the Paramount.

It is, I think, clear that there is a connotation in which the term Ngoni can be used with some degree of scientific accuracy – that is, to cover all those clans which are not belonging to the local tribes, or, in an even stricter sense, the clans of indubitably southern origin.

We have also to recognize that the wider connotation of the word is in constant use today, and it will be apparent in the course of this article that those who like to be thought Ngoni but have no real claim to the name, find ways in which to identify themselves with the real Ngoni, and to impress upon outsiders that they share the distinction of that name." – (bid.).

As a cultural entity, the Ngoni are or exist as a homogeneous unit although it is heterogeneous in terms of origin. As Margaret Read stated on what she found out during her research among the Ngoni:

"It is evident that the field worker who tries to describe and analyse the society which is found in the Ngoni areas today has some difficulty in establishing appropriate and correct terms.

Here is a society which is a compound of ethnic units, subdivided into clans according to kinship, stratified into ranks, held together by a ruling aristocracy and a strong centralized political organization. This society differs radically from that of a homogeneous community where the sociological structure has gone through a long process of integration or disintegration, or has remained static over a period of time.

The Ngoni created their 'state,' that is, their present political and social units, within a relatively short period by a series of deliberate acts. They brought with them a pattern of society from the south; they modified it during their forty odd years of wandering and warfare; and they moulded it finally when they settled in their present areas. Within this deliberately created social structure the principles of centralization and rank were dominant.

Based on these two principles the Ngoni set up, in an alien milieu, the institutions of chieftainship, of military training, of systematized law courts, of recognized ranks in society, of patrilineal succession and inheritance, speaking among themselves a language foreign to the country. The resultant society, a compound of the Ngoni ruling aristocracy and the conquered indigenous people, formed the Ngoni state.

So conscious was all this social engineering that old men today can give detailed accounts of the various processes, political, legal, military, by which the conquerors and conquered were brought under one rule.

Borrowing a term from European history, it might almost be called nation-building. And when you have heard the Ngoni Paramount discuss the position of minorities in his country, and his claim to territories no longer under his rule, you could almost imagine you were in the corridors of the League Secretariat at Geneva.

The Ngoni state, however, today is not only a political structure, a framework for political and social life. Within that structure, forming parts of it, are institutions embodying those social, political, economic, and ethical values which are peculiarly Ngoni. The Ngoni, that is to say, when they absorbed other peoples into their state, imposed upon them a new social order together with the values inherent in that order.

Patrilineal succession and inheritance, for example, introduced by the Ngoni, was bound up with the relations of father to son, the acquiring and distribution of cattle, the worship of clan and family ancestors.

Each institution had its clearly related rules and values, and these are made explicit by the Ngoni when they describe them.

The casual European observer in the country sees only the Paramount Chief and his subordinate chiefs ruling over a welter of tribes with a confusing mixture of social behaviour. To the Ngoni, however, and to the anthropologist who follows their lead, the pattern of society which they set up is clear and definite; it has a cultural reality of its own.

The seeming welter of tribes is in reality an ordered relationship. Each group, tribe, or clan, has its recognized place vis-a-vis other groups. Within that ordered relationship the different groups have pursued a process of preserving some customs and adopting others, and they can give a coherent account of what they have retained and what they have borrowed.

The real Ngoni do not admit to borrowing much. They like to think of their society as very distinctive as well as being well integrated.

Yet the degree of modification in Ngoni society needs very close investigation because it shows much variety in different localities.

When they entered their present areas the Ngoni were very inferior in numbers to the indigenous people. How was it then that they were able to subdue them? And having subdued them, how did they preserve their own culture, so that they were not submerged in the very different cultures round them?

The Ngoni themselves give the answer to this first question, saying, 'We fought with spears and shields; those others had only bows and arrows and sometimes guns.' The making of these shields, which formerly gave courage and protection to the warriors, is to this day almost a ritual. To watch a chief working at one on the threshold of his hut, or a village headman and his friends cutting and shaping one in the kraal, is to realize the value put on them by the Ngoni. They refuse to make them for sale as curiosities, and several Europeans have told me that they have tried in vain to get one.

Having conquered by the shield and spear, the Ngoni maintained their prestige by their highly developed political organization. All around them were small chieftains owning a few villages with no integration in any large political unit. The Ngoni state was focussed in the *inkosi*, the Paramount Chief, who was at once the 'owner' of the land, the 'head' of the state, and the 'father' of his people.

The Ngoni, as we have seen, are always ready to indicate those institutions and related traditions which mark them off from the surrounding tribes, and which give their state a cultural reality of its own.

They point first to their language and their traditions of Dingiswayo, Zwidi, and Chaka as proving their southern origin. Other neighbouring peoples have vague traditions of wandering from north to south, or west to east, but the Ngoni know exactly where they came from and by what route. Their language is almost identical with old Zulu. I was told by many Europeans that it hardly existed any longer, and I was therefore surprised to find to what an extent it is still spoken and used.

Most of the true Ngoni today are bilingual; with the exception of a few very old Ngoni people, everyone today speaks one of the local vernaculars, Nsenga, Tumbuka, or Chewa.

Ngoni is the language of the aristocrats, and a large proportion of the true Ngoni understand and speak it. It is in fact one of the distinguishing marks between the true Ngoni and the rest. It is convenient for a chief to be able to exchange a few remarks with a relative or an important visitor in a language which the onlookers cannot follow, and I have also heard a chief do the same with one of his *indunas* during a case in court.

When I played Zulu records on my gramophone the aristocrats and old warriors drew near to listen, while the nobodies who could not understand fell back naturally.

It is interesting to see how this language test brings out the social distinctions based on family and rank, and produces generally an inferiority reaction among the non-Ngoni." – (Ibid.).

She went on to state:

"As other distinguishing institutions the Ngoni point out their dances and songs; their former military organization with its related system of age grades; their political organization under the Paramount Chief with his hierarchy of *amakosana, abalumuzana, izinduna, amanxusa*; the system of courts, again a hierarchy, with the laws administered in them; their village organization which still preserves the division into *izigawa* or hamlets, characteristic of the very big Ngoni villages of old days; the Ngoni code of ethics, differing radically from the code of the neighbouring tribes, with its insistence on truth, chastity, and personal discipline; and their patrilineal descent in clans and inheritance of property. This last, superimposed upon the local matrilineal and matrilocal tribes, has created a variety of forms of marriage and inheritance which is almost the despair of the field worker.

The Ngoni say proudly, 'We taught them to honour their sons' when pointing out how nephew succession has to a large extent given way before filial succession.

The values inherent in certain Ngoni institutions have spread beyond their own areas, for one Chewa Paramount Chief told me he had for long admired the Ngoni system of filial succession and inheritance, and was now trying, in the teeth of much opposition, to introduce it into his country.

After I had been a little while among the Ngoni, and their chiefs and leading men had begun to realize my aim in field work, I was surprised by the help they gave me and the amount of cooperation they showed in my enquiries. Then one day an old *induna* revealed the reason for this enthusiasm about being 'written up.' 'At last,' he said, 'someone will know about us.'

He went on to speak with regret about the old days when one or two missionaries and others really knew about the Ngoni and could speak their language. He then spoke with bitterness about the present, lamenting that the Ngoni were no longer regarded as a great people.

Gradually it became evident that the Ngoni, being very conscious themselves of their distinctive cultural identity, and of their positive achievements in setting up the Ngoni state, expect other people to recognize this too. They keep constantly before them memories of their past greatness, and they dwell gloomily on the coming of the Europeans which marked the end of their ascendancy." – (Ibid.).

Like most ethnic groups in Africa, the Ngoni do exist but not as a "pure" ethnic entity whose members are united only by a single common ancestry in terms of origin, traced to one ancestor. They are united by historical and cultural-linguistic ties. There are no "pure" tribes.

I have looked at Ngoni society in some detail, more than I have other groups in Malawi, because it is one of the best examples of state formation or nation building in Africa in precolonial times like the Ashanti, the Baganda, the Bakongo, the Yoruba and the Zulu, of course, among many others.

Tumbuka

Like the Ngoni, the Tumbuka are another ethnic group which straddles national boundaries.

In Malawi, the Tumbuka live mostly in the northern part of the country. In Tanzania they live in the southwestern part, and in the Zambia, they live in the northeastern part of the country.

Their language is closely related to the languages of their neighbours – the Tonga, the Chewa and the Senga. It has also incorporated some Swahili elements because of contact with Arab and African slave traders from the coast and proximity of Malawian Tumbuka territory to Tanzania where Swahili is the main language and where many Tumbukas also live.

Like most Malawians, they are mostly farmers. They are also migrant workers and live in other countries in the region. They are some of the people who were conquered by the Ngoni. They also suffered the ravages of the slave trade by the Arabs. A lot of intermarriage took place between the Ngoni and Tumbuka, resulting in a hybrid culture although it is essentially Tumbuka with its own distinct identity.

The history of the Tumbuka, like the histories of other ethnic groups, is replete with oral traditions to authenticate different claims including the origin of the people involved. In the case of Malawi, there is even a claim that the people who currently occupy the country have ties to the land dating back centuries, in spite of the fact that there are some groups, such as the Ngoni, who are relatively new and can be classified as recent arrivals. As Colin Baker states in his book, *Chipembere: The Missing Years*:

"According to oral history and to the writings of

contemporary historians some of whom we have already quoted, practically every tribe now found in Malawi is of ancient Malawi stock.

John McCracken in the book and chapter already mentioned, excludes Ngonde of the northern tip of Malawi from the list of original Malawi tribes and says their affinities were more with East African tribes than with the people of ancient Malawi.

This is a point on which I have done no research or oral investigation and cannot support or refute the statement with my present limited knowledge. But if we remember the point made earlier, that the Malawi Kingdom experienced periods of expansion as well as periods of shrinkage, we will no doubt realise that the possibility of the Ngonde or any other tribe having been at one time part of the Malawi Kingdom and at another part of one of the neighbouring kingdoms, is great indeed. In other words, there were no precise boundaries.

Moreover, Malawi is a compact, densely populated country. No people live in a kind of 'tribal island,' clearly separated from the rest geographically. There is much overlapping of tribal areas. No area is inhabited entirely by people of one tribe only. The total population is small but the number of people per square mile is among the highest in Africa.

This compactness, and the fact of the people living close together, has resulted in extensive intermarriage between tribes, with the result that today there are hardly any Malawians who can claim to have the blood of only one tribe in their veins. One example is Dr. Banda (the first president of Malawi) whose mother was Chewa and whose father was Tumbuka by language and Ngoni by tribe and had moved to Dr. Banda's home district of Kasungu from the neighbouring Mzimba District.

So if there are, in Malawi, tribes that were originally not of Malawi stock they have acquired Malawi blood through intermarriage." – (Colin Baker, *Chipembere: The*

Missing Years, Zomba, Malawi: Kachere Series, Kachere Books No. 25, 2008, p. 256).

He goes on to state:

"But McCracken is quite right when he says that the Tumbuka-speaking people are of original Malawi stock. Not only is there an oral tradition which states that they have close blood affinities with the other Malawi tribes; they also have similarity of clan names with the latter. Thus one finds that while the Tonga people have such clan names as Phiri, Banda, Mwase, etc. which are found extensively among the Chewa, the Tumbuka people have such clan names as Nyirenda, Kaunda, Longwe, etc. which are very common among the Tonga people.

In addition, the Tumbuka and Tonga languages are so similar that a speaker using one of these languages can be understood fully by an audience consisting of people whose mother tongue is the other language.

Oral history also claims common origins between the Tumbuka-speaking people of Malawi and eastern Zambia on the one hand, and the Senga people of south-eastern Zambia whose Malawi origins are not in dispute, on the other; and similarity in accent and intonation tends to confirm this claim, while some of the Senga words are similar to those found in the Chi-Nyanja language.

It is also common knowledge that in pre-Ngoni invasion days the Tumbuka-speaking people extended further to the south of the place where they are found now, but were forced to move further north by the A-Ngoni invasion and settlement. They might have had to move a little further had they not put up a stout and heroic resistance in the famous battle of Mount Hora.

Admittedly, there are Tumbuka-speaking families or villages that consist of what are called 'Barowoka,' descendants of groups of people who had been living on the eastern shores and had crossed to the western side of the lake where they are found to-day; but they are a minority and have intermarried extensively with the Tumbuka people they found when they arrived on the western side." – (Ibid., pp. 256 – 257).

The history of the Tumbuka is one of intermingling with members of other groups, besides the Ngoni, the Chewa, and the Tonga, and establishment of political and social institutions which are a product of such interaction:

"The contemporary Tumbuka are the offspring of a complex intermingling of people of diverse origins. The original inhabitants of the area, mostly matrilineal in descent, lived in highly scattered homesteads and had a weak, decentralized political organization.

In the late 18th century a group of traders involved in the East African ivory trade arrived in the area and established a string of politically centralized chiefdoms among the Tumbuka in an attempt to control the region's export trade in ivory. Their rule collapsed about 1855, when the Tumbuka area was subjugated by a group of Ngoni, a highly militarized refugee people from South Africa.

The intermingling of the Tumbuka with their Ngoni overlords resulted in great cultural changes for both. The Tumbuka adopted the compact villages, patrilineal descent, and dance and marriage customs of the Ngoni, while the Ngoni adopted the Tumbuka agricultural system and the Tumbuka language. By 1900 the Ngoni language was effectively in disuse, and the Tumbuka-speaking group had abandoned many elements of its original culture.

This situation began to change with the imposition of British colonial rule in the 1890s. As the prestige of the Ngoni declined under the impact of British administration in the area, the Tumbuka began to reassert their traditional culture and form independent villages. Tumbuka dances and religious practices were revived, and in the 20th century the Tumbuka became a notable example of reborn ethnic consciousness." – ("Tumbuka People," *Encyclopaedia Britannica*).

Like members of other ethnic groups, the Tumbuka played an important role in the formation of the Nyasaland African Congress, transformed into the Malawi Congress Party which led the country to independence in 1964:

"The Tumbuka were among the first to establish political organizations to oppose the British colonial system. Under the leadership of such men as Levi Mumba and Charles Chinula, Tumbuka speakers were in the fore of early nationalist movements, which in the 1940s coalesced to form the Nyasaland African Congress.

Since the independence of Malaŵi in 1964, the political power of the Tumbuka speakers has been eroded. Northern Malaŵi and eastern Zambia remain poverty-stricken and lack exploitable natural resources.

The Tumbuka people still practice subsistence hoe agriculture, and their incomes are supplemented by the earnings sent home by migrant workers outside the Tumbuka area." – (Ibid.).

Also like other Malawians, the Tumbuka are mostly Christian but still practise traditional religious beliefs based on the existence of a Supreme Being who was self-created and knows everything, a religious and philosophical concept that underlies many traditional religions across Africa. Communicating with departed ancestors is one of the central components of their traditional religious beliefs; so is spirit possession.

Their beliefs and traditional way of life are not fundamentally different from those of other groups in Malawi and even in many other parts of Africa, especially in the neighbouring countries of Tanzania and Zambia.

This validates their common identity – of all these diverse ethnic entities – as "one people" in a region where members of different groups live transcending national boundaries which were created by Europeans when they carved out territories across the continent during the partition of Africa to satisfy their greed and imperial ambitions.

Before European came, Africa was one in the sense that the people were free to move from one place to another, traversing vast expanses of territory – hundreds and even thousands of miles – and settle where they wanted to settle without being asked along the way, "where are you going, where did you come from, who allowed you to come into our country – let alone where is your passport?"

In the context of Malawi, the one-ness of the people was expressed by Baker in the following words in his book, *Chipembere: The Missing Years*:

"For us as a nation, the important point is that, through historical forces beyond our control, Malawi, our country, consists of those lands which the British empire founders carved out of Africa and named 'Nyasaland.' For weal or for woe, our nation will always consist of those lands and their people.

Any hope that we can in this 20th century expand our territory at the expense of our neighbours is as tragic an illusion as to think that we can afford to break up into small tribal nationalities or become a nation dominated or governed by one tribe. We cannot reverse the wheels of history.

The lessons of the Congo, Nigeria-Biafra, and Sudan are highly tragic but are in a sense beneficial to the rest of Africa. We can ignore them only at our own peril.

Destiny or Fate has brought us, the people of Malawi, together within our present boundaries; within these boundaries let us for ever remain together and for ever be content." – (op. cit., p. 257).

Sena

The Sena are probably the most prominent group in Malawi to demonstrate that "indigenous" people are not the only ones who can claim to be "true" Malawians.

They migrated to Nyasaland, now Malawi, only recently contrasted with other people including the Ngoni who are also immigrants but arrived much earlier before the Sena did.

The Sena migrated from northwestern Mozambique and settled in Nyasaland in the early 1900s. They also settled in Southern Rhodesia, now Zimbabwe, during the same period. They left Mozambique in search of employment as labourers. This migratory trend eventually led to the formation of Sena ethnic entities in both countries significant enough to constitute a new tribe in each of the two countries where they settled.

Like members of other groups, they are not "pure." They are a mixture of different people, yet essentially Shona in terms of culture and even ancestry. The Chewa also have had profound influence on the Sena in terms of culture, an interaction that has also been reinforced by intermarriage and other forms of interaction not just with the Shona and the Chewa but with other people of different ethnic and historical backgrounds. Even their language has many dialects, a phenomenon that may be attributed to a mixture of languages of different groups ethnic groups some of whose members have been integrated into Sena society.

The Sena were also greatly influenced by the Portuguese who settled in their traditional homeland in the Zambezi River valley in Mozambique and ended up adopting some customs and values of these settlers from Europe; a situation similar to what happened in Ghana where the Fante intermingled with the British and other Europeans in the coastal areas – home of the Fante – for a long time. They ended up adopting European ways, making them the most Europeanised people in the country, a cultural assimilation facilitated by intermarriage. Many Fantes are a product of this mixed ancestry.

The Sena also have intermarried with the members of other ethnic groups in the countries where they have settled and even in their ancestral homeland of Mozambique just as other people have.

This was also facilitated by their way of life as migrant labourers after they left Mozambique and mingled with the people of other tribes in the areas where they found employment in Nyasaland and Southern Rhodesia.

The Sena may also have Jewish ancestry because they are related to the Lemba whose identity has been established as an African people who have some Jewish genes. The Sena who live in Nsanje and Chikhwawa districts in southern Malawi are a branch of the Lemba.

The Lemba are scattered in a number of countries but live mostly in the northern part of South Africa and in Zimbabwe, and in smaller numbers in Mozambique. Some may also live in Tanzania as descendants of the original Jewish immigrants – intermarried with Africans – who moved south in their long journey from Sena, Yemen, more than 2,000 years ago. According to the World Jewish Congress in its article, "Lemba tribe in southern Africa has Jewish roots, genetic tests reveal":

"Genetic tests carried out by British scientists have revealed that many of the Lemba tribesmen in southern Africa have Jewish origins, according to a report by the BBC. The Lemba, a tribe of 70,000 to 80,000 members who live in central Zimbabwe and northern South Africa, have customs which are similar to Jewish ones: Lemba refrain from eating pork or other foods forbidden by the Torah, or forbidden combinations of permitted foods, wear yarmulke-like skull caps, conduct ritual animal slaughter, have a holy day once a week, and even put a Star of David on their gravestones. According to their oral tradition, the Lemba are descended from seven Jewish men who left Israel 2,500 years ago and married African women, according to the BBC. The Lemba prefer their children to marry other Lembas, and marriage to non-Lembas is being discouraged.

Their sacred prayer language is a mixture of Hebrew and Arabic. Their religious artifact is a replica of the Biblical Ark of the Covenant known as the 'ngoma lungundu', meaning "the drum that thunders." The object went on display recently at a museum in Harare, Zimbabwe, and has instilled pride in many of the Lemba. They say the ark was built almost 700 years ago from the remains of the original ark, which according to the Bible was used to store the Ten Commandments. For decades, the ancient vessel was thought to be lost until it was discovered in a storeroom in Harare recently.

Members of the priestly clan of the Lemba, the Buba – which is one of 12 clans – have a genetic element also found among the Jewish priestly line, known as Kohanim. "This was amazing," Professor Tudor Parfitt from the University of London told the BBC. 'It looks as if the Jewish priesthood continued in the West by people called Cohen, and in same way it was continued by the priestly clan of the Lemba.'

Despite their roots, many of the tribe are now Christians or Muslims." – (World Jewish Congress, "Lemba tribe in southern Africa has Jewish roots, Genetic Tests Reveal," 8 March 2010).

The Tonga practise the same religious beliefs and may also have Jewish ancestry. As one commentator, Miyoba Sichimwi, stated on 22 May 2017 when commenting on the article about Lemba's Jewish roots on the World Jewish Congress website:

"Interesting and insightful.

There is also a tribe or group of tribes in southern Zambia called Tonga, they also seem similar to the Lemba tribe attributes, they are predominately Sabbath keeping, a holy day once a week, ritual slaughter of cattle, they do not consume unclean meats as per Mosiac laws and very united, in that they also encourage marriage amongst themselves.

Please can you investigate and ascertain if they are part of the lost tribes of Israeal, as the Lemba, I have feeling they are too. There are no coincidences in such matters."

Another reader, using the name May, stated the following on the same website on 4 August 2017 in response to what Miyoba Sichimwi wrote about the Tonga:

"Miyoba Sichimwi, just to add on to what you said.

Our great-grand parents told us (oral tradition) about some of the Lemba tribe (they were being mistreated) that crossed over to Zambia, and southern province, and had Zimbabwean names which later the names got to mix with the Tonga names. They intermarried with the Tongas.

These people reached as far as Mazabuka. There is still one who is alive in Husband's village who can tell you the whole story.

What you are saying about the SDA group in Zambia could be true and true of other Tonga's who are not SDA.

I believe we have Jewish blood! Someone needs to go to Zambia, that southern part and test more especially our old people who are still alive!"

Peter Ng'oma Phiri had this to say on 27 May 2017 about the Sena and others on the possibility they may have Jewish ancestry:

"Wonderful and it's great because to find gold you have to dig up.

Now how about this people Sena and Mang'anja found in south Malawi are they not from the same tribe (group) they also have the same manor (manner). They do slaughter animals when they want meat and have one holy day a week."

Thabi, on 9 March 2017, had this:

"The Lemba and the Ibu people confirm the history of the Bakgalaka (northern Sotho) and Bakalanga (Isindebele) who travelled from Ethiopia and arrived in Zimbabwe after escaping prosecution from forced Christianity and who crossed over to South Africa and were once again forced to leave their traditions of Hebrew nature to adopt Christianity.

Many indeed became Lutheran, Roman Catholic and some chiefs refused to convert. Those who converted still practised their traditional rituals during functions such as weddings, and child naming.

Most settled in the northern province and today the DNA tests agree with the history."

Even if the Sena and the Tonga as well as others – such as the Venda who are close to the Lemba – do indeed have Jewish ancestry, it does not mean they are Jews. They are black Africans more than anything else and simply have other ancestries – Jewish as well as ancestries of other African groups and maybe even others.

They have their own distinct identities as African ethnic groups like their fellow countrymen – and women – in Malawi. Their histories also demonstrate, once again, that there are no "pure" tribes or "pure" people anywhere on earth.

That is why there is not a single Malawian – Zambian, Zimbabwean or any other African – who has the bloodline of just one "pure" tribe. And probably none is trying to run away from his/her African identity and claim to be non-black.

Claims of Jewish ancestry by black people – as well as others – is nothing new. Even President Leopold Sedar Senghor of Senegal said he had Jewish ancestry. But he was not trying to run away from his blackness or his African identity and heritage. He was a leading proponent of Negritude, in fact the most prominent one. As George E. Lichtblau, an American diplomat of Jewish ancestry, stated in his article, "Jewish Roots in Africa":

"Claims of a historic presence of Jewish communities in certain regions of Africa, notably West and Southern Africa, seem esoteric when first mentioned. This presence goes back not just centuries, but even to biblical times.

Of course in two areas such a communal presence on the African continent remains a firmly acknowledged part of Jewish history and experience (North Africa and Egypt/Ethiopia).

A Jewish presence in Egypt and the former Kingdom of Kush are described in the Book of Exodus. Yet even after their exodus from Egypt and their settlement in the land of Israel, the Jewish tribes retained certain nomadic characteristics which are reflected throughout their history....

But the subsequent scattering of a Jewish presence and influence reaching deep into the African continent is less widely acknowledged.

Pressed under sweeping regional conflicts, Jews settled as traders and warriors in Yemen, the Horn of Africa, Egypt, the Kingdom of Kush and Nubia, North African Punic settlements (Carthage and Velubilis), and areas now covered by Mauritania.

More emigrants followed these early Jewish settlers to Northern Africa following the Assyrian conquest of the Israelites in the 8th century B.C.E., and again 200 years later, when Jerusalem was conquered by the Babylonians, leading to the destruction of the First Temple.

This catastrophic event not only drove many Jews into exile in Babylon, but also led to the establishment of exile communities around the Mediterranean, including North Africa.

Then, with Israel coming under Greek, Persian and later Roman rule and dependence, renewed waves of Jewish traders and artisans began to set up communities in Egypt, Cyrenaica, Nubia and the Punic Empire, notably in Carthage, whence they began to scatter into various newly emerging communities south of the Atlas mountains.

Several Jewish nomadic groups also started to come across the Sahara from Nubia and the ancient kingdom of Kush.

The Jewish presence in Africa began to expand significantly in the second and third centuries of the Christian era, extending not only into the Sahara desert, but also reaching down along the West African coast, and possibly also to some Bantu tribes of Southern Africa (where some 40,000 members of the Lemba tribe still claim Jewish roots).

The names of old Jewish communities south of the Atlas mountains, many of which existed well into Renaissance times, can be found in documents in synagogue archives in Cairo.

In addition, Jewish, Arab and Christian accounts cite the existence of Jewish rulers of certain tribal groups and clans identifying themselves as Jewish scattered throughout Mauritania, Senegal, the Western Sudan, Nigeria, and Ghana.

Among notable Arab historians referring to their existence are Ibn Khaldun, who lived in the 13th century, a respected authority on Berber history; the famous geographer al-Idrisi, born in Ceuta, Spain in the 12th century, who wrote about Jewish Negroes in the western Sudan; and the 16th century historian and traveler Leon

Africanus, a Moslem from Spain who was raised by a Jewish woman working in his family's household, who is said to have taught him Hebrew and emigrated with the family to Morocco in 1492.

Leon Africanus later converted to Catholicism but remained interested in Jewish communities he encountered throughout his travels in West Africa.

Some evidence can also be derived from surviving tribal traditions of some African ethnic groups, including links to biblical ancestors, names of localities, and ceremonies with affinities to Jewish ritual practices. Moreover, the writings of several modern West African historians and two personal anecdotes indicate that the memories of an influential Jewish historical past in West Africa continue to survive.

I still remember from my assignments in the 1960's as a Foreign Service Officer an encounter with Mr. Bubu Hama, then president of the National Assembly in Niger and a prolific writer on African history. He told me that the Tuaregs had a Jewish queen in early medieval times, and that some Jewish Tuareg clans had preserved their adherence to that faith, in defiance of both Islamic and Christian missionary pressure, until the 18th century.

In several of his books Hama even cites some genealogies of Jewish rulers of the Tuareg and Hausa kingdoms.

A related story about surviving memories of Jewish roots in West Africa was told to me around 1976 by former Israeli prime minister Shimon Peres.

He had just returned from a meeting of the Socialist International, during which he had met with then president Leopold Senghor of Senegal. In the course of their discussion about the possibility of normalizing Senegalese-Israeli relations, Senghor had told him that he too had Jewish ancestors. At that time we both smiled somewhat incredulously.

Yet, indeed, there are a number of historical records of

small Jewish kingdoms and tribal groups known as *Beni Israel* that were part of the Wolof and Mandinge communities. These existed in Senegal from the early Middle Ages up to the 18th century, when they were forced to convert to Islam. Some of these claimed to be descendants of the tribe of Dan, the traditional tribe of Jewish gold and metal artisans, who are also said to have built the 'Golden Calf.'

Jewish presence is said to have been introduced into Senegal, Mauritania and numerous other West African countries south of the Sahara in part through the migration of Jewish Berber groups and later through some exiles who had been expelled from Spain, had first settled in North Africa, and had then crossed the Atlas mountains.

Other even earlier arrivals are said to have come from Cyrenaica (now part of Libya, Egypt, the Sudan and Ethiopia), having crossed the Sahara to West Africa and eventually also moved further south.

In addition to the Jewish tribal groups in Senegal who claim to be descendants of the tribe of Dan, the Ethiopian Jews also trace their ancestry to the tribe of Dan.

Some of these transmigrants established communities in such still renowned places as Gao, Timbuktu (where UNESCO still maintains notable archives containing records of its old Jewish community), Bamako, Agadez, Kano and Ibadan.

A notable number of Berber and African nomad tribal groups joined up with the Jewish communal groups trying to resist aggressiqve Arab Islamic efforts or as bulwark against Christian proselytizing, sometimes going so far as to convert to Judaism. Notable among these were some Tuareg, Peul and Ibadiya groups.

Another source at the root of this Jewish presence and influence was the spreading gold trade emanating from Persia, with Jews becoming involved as important intermediary traders. These traders came to rely on contacts with scattered Jewish communities they encountered in their West African travels in search for gold, a trade widely prohibited to Muslims as usurious under Islamic law. Thus, for instance, various historical accounts claim that Jewish travelers from Persia had organized exchanges of Chinese silk for gold in the Kingdom of Ghana; the Ashanti needed the silk for weaving Kente cloth.

To this day it is said that the Ashanti words for numbers relate to those in Parsi, the language of Persia.

Under the impact of this Jewish influence a number of ruling families in Ghana converted to Judaism, and for nearly 200 years the Kingdom of Ghana, which extended at that time far north into western Sudan, was ruled by Jewish kings.

Because of their skills, abilities, and multilingual knowledge, Jews became important intermediaries in regional trade relations and as artisans grouping together as craft guilds. They are said to have formed the roots of a powerful craft tradition among the still-renowned Senegalese goldsmiths, jewelers and other metal artisans. The name of an old Senegalese province called 'Juddala' is said to attest to the notable impact Jews made in this part of the world.

Jewish presence is also confirmed by numerous surviving accounts of Portuguese and other European visitors in the 14th and 15th centuries, as well as North African and Arab historical records.

Gradually most of these communities disappeared. Since they existed largely in isolation, there was a good deal of intermarriage which for a while reinforced their influence and expansion. As a result they were increasingly viewed as a threat by Muslim rulers, and most of the Jewish communities and nomad groups south of the Atlas mountains were either forced to convert to Islam or massacred; the remainder fled to North Africa, Egypt or the Sudan, and a few also to Cameroon and Southern Africa."

Jewish ancestry of other groups in southern Africa besides the Lemba cannot be discounted; nor does it undermine the identity of these groups, including some in Malawi, as black African.

Tonga

The Tonga live mostly in the Northern Region of Malawi. They occupy areas close to Lake Nyasa, especially Nkhata Bay and the northern part of Nkhotakota.

They were conquered by the Ngoni and came under centralised authority which had never been their form of government.

As residents of the shores of Lake Nyasa, they have always relied on fishing as a means to earn a living. They are also farmers.

Their traditional religion is centred on the existence of a Supreme Being who is a mystery. It also includes "ancestor worship" – n communicating with the departed ancestors and seeking guidance from them through spirit mediums.

Some of the most well-known Tonga surnames are Chirwa and Kaunda.

One of the most prominent Chirwas in Malawi was Orton Chirwa who became the country's first minister of justice and attorney-general after the country won independence. He was imprisoned by President Kamuzu Banda and died in prison in 1992. He was on death row for eleven years after being convicted of treason. His wife, Vera Chirwa, was also convicted of treason and spent twelve years on death row.

They were abducted from exile in Zambia in 1981 and returned to Malawi to be tried for treason. They were prisoners of conscience for opposing the tyrannical rule of

President Banda.

And the most prominent Kaunda was a Zambian of Malawian origin: former Zambian president, Kenneth Kaunda, whose father, David Kaunda, came from Nyasaland.

It is also in Zambia where the Tonga stand out as the second-largest ethnic group after the Bemba.

Their history is similar to that of other tribes in terms of intermingling with members of other ethnic groups through the years, leading to formation of ethnic entities which are a product of other tribes as well. This underscores one fundamental fact: All the tribes of Malawi are basically the same people.

The different tribal cultures are basically the same in many fundamental respects and they all – hence the people themselves – have different origins but have ended up merging to form the ethnic groups which exist today. As Daniel Kapenyela Mphande, a Tonga, states in his book, *Oral Literature and Moral Education among the Lakeside Tonga of Northern Malawi*: *A Study of Tonga Culture in Northern Malawi*:

"The Lakeside Tonga people of Malawi, in Nkhata Bay district, share in the Bantu history to which their ancestors belonged....Most historians would see the Tonga people as of heterogeneous origin.

Jan van Velsen has noted that the genesis of the Tonga nation probably lies in the later decades of the 18th century. This was the period of the penetration of ivory trading groups from across the north-eastern shores of Lake Nyasa and the tribal movements in the northern part of what is now Malawi, when some groups settled in Tongaland. As noted earlier, some believe that the Tonga came from the same place as the Chewa and Tumbuka, pointing to Chewa and Tumbuka names found in Chitonga – Phiri, Banda, Mwale, Nkhoma – and to the presence of many similar words.

What seems to be most likely is that the Tonga had good relationships with Tumbuka and Chewa with whom they intermarried....

The process of amalgamation may have been speeded up in the third quarter of the nineteenth century through the external pressure of the Ngoni under Mbelwa. Raided by these Ngoni from the 1850s, the Tonga had retained a tenuous independence by retiring into a number of large, fortified villages instead of living in small scattered villages....

During the frequent Ngoni raids some of the Tonga subjects were taken as captives. In 1881, however, the Ngoni experienced a temporary resurgence of power. Many of their earlier difficulties appear to have risen from the rapid accumulation of these captives, and their failure to assimilate them fully within their society.

According to tradition several Tonga captives distinguished themselves as captains in the Ngoni armies. The state of bondage in which the Tonga lived in Ngoniland did not last long. In the middle of the 1870s the Tonga rose in revolt and decamped to the lakeshore where they were received in the *malinga* (stockades) and elsewhere. The pursuing Ngoni were routed in the battle of the Lueya River around Chintheche by Mankhambira's stockade....

This early interaction between Ngoni and Tonga had an important impact on the Ngoni culture. Those Tonga who were under Ngoni captivity for about twenty-five years, obviously intermarried. This explains why names like Chirwa, Kamanga, Phiri, Mphande, and so on, are common in Ngoniland. By living in the stockades, the Tonga learnt to live together in harmony. Here family relations and marriages were strengthened, chiefships were expanded to clans and so on." – (Daniel Kapenyela Mphande, *Oral Literature and Moral Education among the Lakeside Tonga of Northern Malawi*: *A Study of Tonga Culture in Northern Malawi*, Luwinga, Mzuzu, Malawi:

Mzuni Press, 2014, pp. 53, 54, 55 – 56).

He goes on to state the following about Tonga culture and way of life:

"The Tonga live in small clusters of houses scattered all over the dambos, the hillsides and by the lakeshore. Most villages are small, often 50 to 80 houses. These grouped compact clusters of thatched huts and some iron-roofed houses constitute Tonga villages.

The villages are the most common settings for the various stories told by the men and women as they sit relaxed by their hamlets in the evenings....

The distribution of the population is determined by the geographical features of Tongaland. Along parts of the lakeshore the population is more concentrated than in the hill regions. As one gets farther inland from the lakeshore plains, the population becomes less concentrated, and the distance between one group of hamlets and another may be greater.

The villages are reached by steep winding paths up which both visitors and residents must negotiate to reach their settled community at the top, and which the women travel many times daily with their water containers balanced on their heads from a well, a running stream or a borehole below the hill. Kabunduli and Timbiri areas are typical of such features.

The staple food of the Tonga is cassava....The Tonga also raise cattle, goats and sheep. There are some cash crops of minor importance such as rice, groundnuts, bananas, maize, tobacco, millet, coffee and tea. Most of the millet, coffee and tea are cultivated in the hills.

The lake area is better supplied with fish, some of which finds its market in the hill area, and as far as the city of Mzuzu." – (Ibid., pp. 56 – 57).

It is a simple rural life typical of most Malawians and

other Africans across the continent.

Ngonde

The Ngonde live mostly in Karonga District in northern Malawi. Just across the border with Tanzania are their brethren, the Nyakyusa, who are also known as Bangonde, a term used to identify those who live in Kyela District which was once a part of Rungwe District that was the home of all Nyakyusa. In fact, the Ngonde of Malawi and the Nyakyusa of Kyela and Rungwe districts belong to the same tribe. They are all Nyakyusa. The Ngonde of Malawi are also known as Nyakyusa.

The Nyakyusa are one of about 170 tribes which were were split by colonial boundaries, separating the people when the colonial rulers formed the countries which exist on the African continent today.

They are related to the Ndali who also straddle the Malawian-Tanzanian border and are basically the same people. Even their languages are mutually intelligible. They also have same tribal names, especially first names; for example, *Anangisye*, *Anyingisye*. Ndali names and Nyakyusa names also have exactly the same meaning.

The Ndali are believed to be a branch of the Nyakyusa. The two separated when they arrived in Rungwe District in southwestern Tanzania about 500 years ago from Mahenge in eastern Tanzania. The Ndali moving west and settled in the mountains; others moved farther south to what is now northern Malawi. Some of the Nyakyusa slso moved farther south and settled in what is now Karinga District.

The Nyakyusa are also related to the Kinga who are their neighbours and live east of Nyakyusaland in Tanzania, and to the Luguru and Pogoro in Morogoro Region in eastern Tanzania where they originated. Some Nyakyusa groups in Rungwe District today even identify themselves as Lugulu. There is no "r" in Nyakyusa language; it is replaced by "l." Hence Lugulu instead of Luguru. And as Bastian Personhn states in his book, *The Verb in Nyakyusa: A Focus in Tense, Aspect and Modality*:

"Nyakyusa is a Bantu language spoken in the Mbeya Region of south-western Tanzania, in the coastal plains of Lake Nyasa (Lake Malawi) and the hills extending to the north of it, with the biggest urban centres being Tukuyu and Kyela. Its homeland forms part of the so-called Nyasa-Tanganyika Corridor and is characterized by heavy rainfall and fertile ground.

The Ethnologue estimates 1,080,000 speakers in Tanzania (Simons & Fenning 2017), while Muzale &Rugemalira (2008) give a number of 732,990.

Nyakyusa is vigorously used by all generations and also learned by local non-native speakers. Most speakers are bilingual in Swahili. Nyakyusa is surrounded by other Bantu languages, among the Kinga to the east, Kisi to the southeast, and Safwa and Wanji in the north. Its closest relatives are Ngonde, spoken further (sic) south in Malawi and Ndali.

Nyakyusa and Ngonde are typically treated as one language. However, the limited data available on Malawian Ngonde points towards major structural divergences....

The linguistic and cultural closeness of Nyakyusa and Ndali is reflected in a shared myth of origin. According to this myth, Ndali and Nyakyusa were part of one ethnic group originating in Mahenge, halfway between their current homelands and the coast. The Ndali people took the longer path, thus the name Ndali (meaning) 'long' (in Ndali and Nyakyusa). A different myth, however, sees a common origin with the Kinga, a group with whom an important cult is shared....

Originally, *Nyakyusa* designated a local chiefdom, and was extended to name all the peoples living north of the

Konde and their closely related mutually intelligible language varieties. The name Nyakyusa relates to a legendary chief Mwakyusa, whose name again is matronym 'son of Kyusa.' The prefix *nya-* designates group, clan or family membership and is a widespread Bantu element. From tha period onwards all linguistic publications dealing with Tanzanian varieties speak of Nyakyusa." – (Bastian Personhn, *The Verb in Nyakyusa: A Focus in Tense, Aspect and Modality*, Berlin, Germany: Language Science Press, 2017, pp.1 – 2, and 3).

It is clear that as an ethnic group, the Nyakyusa have incorporated into their entity elements from other groups and are related to them in many fundamental respects; a phenomenon typical of other tribes across the continent. This applies not only to the Nyakyusa in Tanzania but to their kith-and-kin, the Ngonde, in Malawi.

There are other groups within the Nyakyusa, with some differences here and there but not enough to designate them as distinct or separate entities in terms of ethnicity. They are all basically Nyakyusa.

But there are neighbours who, although very close to the Nyakyusa, are separate ethnic groups with their own distinct identities. They include the Kinga and the Safwa. And as Godfrey Wilson, a renowned British anthropologist who studied the Nyakyusa in the 1930s with his wife Monica Wlilson who was a professor of social anthropology at the University of Cape Town, stated in "The Nyakyusa of South-Western Tanganyika":

"The name Nyakyusa is nowadays used by themselves as a general name for all those who have similar speech and customs and who live in Tanganyika; but formerly it only covered those who live in the south of the district (Rungwe), in the plain and up in the hills as far north as the administrative capital, Tukuyu, and it is still thus used to distinguish this group from others. This group will here be referred to as 'Nyakyusa proper.'

Those in the north of the district to the west and east of Mount Rungwe call themselves *Kukwe* and *Lugulu*, respectively; to the east, under the Livingstone Mountains, is a group of chiefdoms called *Selya*, and farther south, on the north-east corner of the lake (Nyasa), are the *Saku*.

All these five groups share a common culture, distinguished by minor local peculiarities or dialect and custom.

Immediately bordering the Nyakyusa to the south-west are the *Ngonde* – Europeanized as 'Konde' – in Northern Nyasaland; they belong to the same cultural group, but are distinguished by greater differences of custom and speech than the others.

In the hills to the west of the Rift (Valley) live the *Ndali* and the *Lambya*, who are included in this administrative district (of Rungwe); on the plateau under these hills to the west of the Kukwe live the *Penja*, and on the shore of the lake live the *Kisi*, famous as fisherman and potters.

These small groups have languages of their own which, though related to that of the Nyakyusa, are more or less unintelligible to them; and they have equally distinct cultures. But they are now rapidly being assimilated to the Nyakyusa both in speech and in law.

I use the name Nyakyusa, in accordance with modern usage, to include the Nyakyusa proper, the Kukwe, Lugulu, Selya, and Saku groups, but to exclude the Ndali, the Penja, Kisi, and Ngonde....

The Lugulu are called *Mwamba* by the people of Selya; the application of this term, which may be translated 'the hill people, varies from place to place, as also does the application of *Ngonde*." – (Godfrey Wilson, "The Nyakyusa of South-Western Tanganyika," in Elizabeth Colson, Max Gluckman, eds., *Seven Tribes of British Central Africa*, London: Oxford University Press, 1951; Manchester: Manchester University Press, 1959, pp. 254 –

255).

Mwamba means "hill" and the people who live in the northern part of Rungwe District – before it was divided into Kyela and Rungwe – which is mountainous unlike the flatland of Kyela – are called, by the people of Kyela, *Ba-Mwamba*, meaning "people of the hills" or "hill people"; the prefix *ba-* meaning "of." And the people of Kyela are called, by their brethren of the hills in the north, *Ba-Ngonde*. Or *Ba-Ntebela*.

The terms are sometimes considered to be pejorative, depending on the context in which they are used.

I write this from experience and from my knowledge of the subject as a Nyakyusa, an ethnic group that also serves as a bridge between Malawi and Tanzania since members of this tribe are found on both sides of the border.

Had there been no partition of Africa – into British Central Africa (BCA), renamed Nyasaland and then Malawi, and Deutsch-Ostafrika (German East Africa), renamed Tanganyika, and now Tanzania – the Nyakyusa would not have been split up into two "tribes." They would not even have considered themselves to be "different" from each other.

There was even a time when the Nyakyusa of Karonga and of Kyela worked together as one people. The imperial powers ended all that when they divided and separated them. In fact, it was Europeans who, even before the partition of Africa, named the Nyakyusa of Malawi "Konde," a term that acquired legitimacy through the years but which is also an indictment of imperial rule.

Although the colonial powers partitioned the continent and even separated some families when they split up some tribes and restricted their movement, confining them and members of other tribes within their newly-formed countries which became colonies, they did not and could not destroy the identity of Africans as one people.

The people of Malawi are an integral part of the larger

family of the Bantu, an ethno-cultural-linguistic community of the indigenous people whom inhabit East, Central and Southern Africa. Just as transnational groups such as the Ngonde-Nyakyusa, Tumbuka, and Ndali and Lambya who straddle the Malawi-Tanzania border, and the Yao the Malawi-Mozambique border as well as other groups whose identity transcends national boundaries, the people of Malawi form a bridge, a natural bridge, between the people of eastern and southern Africa.

One of the most common features of their common identity as one and the same people – in a Pan-African context – is the similarities in their languages, a linguistic affinity that points to a common origin of these people. For example, the word *kanyama*, which was the name of Malawi's first minister of foreign affairs Kanyama Chiume, means "a small piece of meat" in his native Tonga language; it means exactly the same thing in Ngonde-Nyakyusa and in Swahili. As Godfrey Mwakikagile, a Tanzanian scholar and writer, states in his book, *South Africa as a Multi-Ethnic Society*:

"Members of different Bantu ethnic groups...moved southward from East-Central Africa and spoke related languages. That is why they came to be known as 'Bantu.' It is a linguistic term and simply means 'people' in most of the languages spoken by the members of these ethnic groups. There is no Bantu race.

Let's take Kiswahili or Swahili, the most widely spoken African language – in terms of the numbers of countries which use it – as an example. In Kiswahili, *mtu* means "person," and *watu* means 'people' or 'persons.'

And in Kinyakyusa or Nyakyusa, a language spoken by more than one million people who constitute one of the largest ethnic groups in Tanzania (there are also hundreds of thousands of Nyakyusa people in Malawi who are also called Ngonde or Bangonde), *mundu* means 'person,' and *abandu* or *bandu* means 'people'; a term very close to

Bantu. Terms similar to that are found in other Bantu languages.

And there are many other similarities. The terms *lenja ifile* which gained notoriety in May 2008 when they were uttered by some black South Africans who burned two Mozambicans alive – one miraculously survived while the other one died – immediately come to mind as one of those examples.

The Zulu and other black South Africans say *lenja ifile*, meaning 'the dog is dead.'

The Nyakyusa of Tanzania and Malawi, in the Nyakyusa language which I spoke in Tanzania for many years as I did Swahili, would say *imbwa jifwile*, which means the same thing as *lenja ifile*: 'the dog is dead.' In Swahili, the same expression is slightly different, *mbwa amekufa*, 'the dog is dead.'

Thus, you have a language in East Africa, Nyakyusa, which has striking similarities to a language or languages spoken by black South Africans. And so do many others, and vice versa.

There are many other similarities. For example, the Zulu say *amandhla*, which means 'power.' The Nyakyusa say *amaka*, which also means 'power.' The emphasis in Nyakyusa, as in Zulu, is on the second syllable.

The Zulu, the Ndebele and the Xhosa also say *amanza*, meaning 'water.' The Nyakyusa say *amisi* – emphasis on the second syllable – which means 'water' in Nyakyusa language.

Another example: the Zulu say *ngiphuma*, meaning 'I'm from'; the Nyakyusa say *ngufuma*, which also means, 'I'm from.'

And the language of the Nyakyusa people is called *ikiNyakyusa*. That's what the Nyakyusa call their language, while the Zulu call theirs *isiZulu*, the Ndebele call their language *isiNdebele*, the Xhosa call theirs *isiXhosa* as do other black South Africans who also use the prefix *isi-* in their tribal languages.

And what are the people themselves called in their own languages?

The Nyakyusa are known as *abaNyakyusa* or simply *baNyakyusa* depending on the context in which either of those terms is used. Now look at the similarities.

The Zulu are *amaZulu*, the Xhosa are *amaXhosa*, not very different from *abaNyakyusa*.

And in Nyakyusa language, the Zulu are *abaSulu*, the Xhosa are *abaXhosa*, the Ndebele – *abaNdebele*, and the Swazi – *abaSwasi*, to give only a few examples.

There are no hard consonants in the Nyakyusa language. There's no letter 'z' in Nyakyusa; it is replaced by 's.' Also in Nyakyusa language, there is no letter 'q.' And 'r' is replaced by the letter 'l,' 'v' is replaced by 'f,' and 'w' by 'b' and other letters in different contexts. For example, *watu wengi* is Swahili meaning 'many people.' And *wimbo*, which means 'song' in Swahili, is *lwimbo* in Nyakyusa. But the plural term, *nyimbo*, which means 'songs,' is the same in both languages.

In Swahili 'songs' is *nyimbo*, and in Nyakyusa 'songs' is also *nyimbo*, and *inyimbo*, depending on the context in which the term is used.

Also, among the Nyakyusa, the word for 'father' is *tata*. In Southern Sotho, a language spoken by millions of people in South Africa and which is also the most widely spoken language in the country of Lesotho, the word for 'father' is *ntate*; very little difference between the two – *tata* and *ntate*.

The Nyakyusa also say *batata*, a plural term, which means 'parents' or 'ancestors' depending on the context in which the term is used and exclusively for males. For example, *batata bitu* in Nyakyusa means 'our parents' (male parents) or 'our ancestors' (male ancestors); *batata bosa* means 'all our parents or ancestors,' while *abasukulu* means 'grandparents,' male and female.

And *abasukulu bitu* means "our grandparents" in Nyakyusa.

Mother is *juba* in Nyakyusa, and *bajuba* is the plural term meaning 'mothers,' while *bajuba bitu* means 'our mothers.'

Nkasi gwangu means 'my wife' and *ndume gwangu* means 'my husband' in Nyakyusa. *Abakasi bitu* or *bakasi bitu* means 'our wives,' and *abalume bitu* or *balume bitu* means 'our husbands.' And *abana bitu or bana bitu* means 'our children,' while *mwanangu or mwana gwangu* means 'my child.'

Abana bangu or *bana bangu* means 'my children.'

Mwipwa gwangu means 'my uncle' and *abipwa bitu* means 'our uncles' in Nyakyusa.

Also in Kinyakyusa, a*bakamu bitu* means 'our relatives,' and *abakamu bangu* means 'my relatives.'

Ingamu jangu means 'my name is...' in Nyakyusa, not very much different from Xhosa and Zulu.

The Xhosa and the Zulu say, *igama lam ngu* – 'my name is....'

*Ingamu jako gwe jwani? m*eans 'what's your name?' in Nyakyusa. In Xhosa, it's *Ungubani Igama lakho?* And in Zulu it's *Igama lakho ngubani?* Meaning the same thing, 'what's your name?'

Nangisya injila means 'show me the way' in Nyakyusa. In Xhosa, it's *Ungandikhombisa indlela.* While *injila* means 'way,' in Nyakyusa, it's *indlela* in Xhosa. Very little difference between the two terms.

Even the other two terms, *nangisya* and *Ungandikhombisa,* both of which mean 'show me' in Nyakyusa and Xhosa, respectively, sound similar.

In Nyakyusa, *ilopa* means 'blood.' And *ilopa lyangu* means 'my blood.' But it means more than just the blood that flows in your veins – it also means 'my relative' or 'my relatives'; for example, when the Nyakyusa say *bosa aba ba ilopa lyangu*, which means 'all of these are of my blood.'

And *abandu bitu,* or *bandu bitu,* depending on the context in which *abandu or bandu* is used, means 'our people' in Nyakyusa language.

Abatitu means 'blacks' in Nyakyusa, while *twe batitu* means 'we blacks.' *Tuli batitu* means 'we are black.'

Uswe means 'us' in Nyakyusa, and *umwe* means 'you' in plural form. It can also be used in this context: *Uswe twe baNyakyusa*, a complete sentence meaning 'We Nyakyusa.'

Umwe mwe baXhosa means 'you Xhosa' in Nyakyusa language.

And *abo* means 'those' – for example, when the Nyakyusa say *abandu abo* – means 'those people,' and *abandu aba* means 'these people.'

AbaSulu aba or *aba abaSulu* means 'these Zulu' in Nyakyusa.

AbaNdebele abo or *abo abaNdebele* means 'those Ndebele' in Nyakyusa.

There are more than one million Nyakyusa in Tanzania alone and they are one of the largest ethnic groups or tribes out of 126 in the whole country.

And although there are a lot of similarities between Swahili and other African languages, from which Swahili itself evolved adding Arabic and other foreign words to it, there are still some differences. For example, 'road' in Kiswahili is *barabara*. In Nyakyusa, or Kinyakyusa, the word for 'road' is *nsebo*, and for 'roads' is *misebo*. In Swahili, the plural form is the same – *barabara,* meaning 'roads' just as it means 'road.'

Chakula means 'food' in Swahili or Kiswahili. In Nyakyusa or Kinyakyusa, food is *findu* or *ifindu*.

Mto means 'river' in Swahili; it also means 'pillow.'

In Nyakyusa language, a river is called *lwisi* or *ulwisi*.

Ifilombe or *filombe* means 'maize' in Nyakyusa. In Swahili, 'maize' is *mahindi*.

Unga means 'flour' in Swahili. In Nyakyusa, 'flour' is *ubufu* or *bufu*.

Indima or *ndima* means 'beans' in Nyakyusa. In Swahili, 'beans' is *maharagwe* or *maharage*.

The word for 'lion' in Swahili is *simba*; in Nyakyusa it

is *ingalamu* or *ngalamu*.

Mamba means 'crocodile' in Swahili. In Nyakyusa, 'crocodile' is *ngwina* or *ingwina*.

Swahili for elephant is *tembo*; Nyakyusa – *sofu* or *isofu*.

Swahili for 'python' – *chatu*; Nyakyusa – *sota* or *isota*.

But there are some similarities also. Another word for 'elephant' in Swahili is *ndovu*, clearly derived from Bantu languages and close to the Nyakyusa word *sofu* for 'elephant' but even much closer to those of other Bantu languages.

For example, the Zulu say *ndlovu*, meaning 'elephant'; the Venda of South Africa and southern Zimbabwe say *ndou*, also meaning 'elephant.'

The Venda also say *thoho ya ndou*, meaning 'head of an elephant.' In Swahili it's *kichwa cha ndovu*, and in Nyakyusa, *untu gwa sofu*.

In Bemba, spoken in Zambia, *mutwe ulekalipa* means 'my head is painful' or 'I have a headache.' The term *mutwe* for 'head' is close to the Nyakyusa term *untu* or *ntu* and to the Swahili term *kichwa* all of which mean 'head.' And the word *ntwa* in Nyakyusa means 'headman' or some kind of chief.

The word for 'drum' in Venda is *ngoma*. Also in Swahili, *ngoma* means 'drum' or 'drums.'

The Nyakyusa have a completely different word for that. *Ndingala, or indingala* means 'drum.' Either one can also be used to mean 'drums', in plural form, in Nyakyusa depending on the context in which the term is used.

In Nyakyusa, or ikiNyakyusa as the Nyakyusa call their language, a*balindwana* means 'girls.' In Swahili, the word for 'girls' is *wasichana*, which is completely different from the Nyakyusa word *abalindwana* for 'girls.'

Ilumbu gwako means 'your sister' in Kinyakyusa or Nyakyusa. In Kiswahili or Swahili, *dada yako* means 'your sister.'

Nkasi means 'wife' in Nyakyusa. In Swahili, 'wife' is

99

mke.

Nkasi gwangu or *unkasi gwangu*, depending on the context, means 'my wife' in Nyakyusa. In Swahili, 'my wife' is *mke wangu*.

Mguu means 'leg' and *miguu* means 'legs' in Swahili.

In Nyakyusa, the word for 'leg' is *kilundi*, and for 'legs' is *filundi*.

Mguu wangu means 'my leg' and *miguu yangu* means 'my legs' in Swahili. In Nyakyusa language, 'my leg' is *kilundi kyangu* or *ikilundi kyangu*, and *filundi fyangu* or *ifilundi fyangu* means 'my legs' depending on the context in which *filundi* of *ifilundi* is used.

Indumbula jangu or umojo gwangu means 'my heart' in Nyakyusa. In Kiswahili, *moyo wangu* means 'my heart.'

Nchi yetu means 'our country' or 'our land' in Swahili. The Nyakyusa say *ikisu kyitu*, meaning 'our land.'

Tunakwenda nyumbani kwetu in Kiswahili, or Swahili, means 'we are going to our home,' and *tunakwenda nyumbani* means 'we are going home.'

The Nyakyusa say *tusumwike kukaja kwitu*, meaning 'we are going to our home'; and *tusumwike kukaja* means 'we are going home.'

Twende nyumbani means 'let's go home' in Kiswahili or Swahili. In Kinyakyusa, or Nyakyusa, *tubuke kukaja* means' let's go home.'

Kufuma kugu? It means 'where do you come from?' in Kinyakyusa. In Kiswahili, it's *unatoka wapi?*

Tunsyilile umwipwa gwitu means 'we have buried our uncle' in Kinyakyusa. In Kiswahili, they say, *tumemzika mjomba wetu*. Meaning the same thing.

Asubuhi means 'morning' in Kiswahili. In Kinyakyusa, *lubunju* or *ulubunju* means 'morning.'

Mputi means 'minister, pastor, or preacher' in Nyakyusa, while in Swahili, *mchungaji* means the same thing.

Tusali means 'let's pray' or 'we should pray' in Kiswahili. In Kinyakyusa, *twipute* means 'let's pray' or 'we should pray.'

Mpeli gwitu means 'Our Creator (God)' in Kinyakyusa. Mpeli means 'Creator.' *Kyala* also means 'God' in Nyakyusa. In Swahili, *Mungu* means 'God.'

The word for 'bird' or 'birds' in Kiswahili is *ndege* – the same term is applied to an aeroplane or aeroplanes. In Nyakyusa, 'a bird' is called *injuni or njuni* depending on the context; the same term is also used in plural form. So *njuni* or *injuni* also means 'birds' in Nyakyusa.

The term *njuni* also brings up interesting comparisons in a linguistic context.

The Nyakyusa who are indigenous to southwestern Tanzania close to the border with Malawi call birds, *njuni* or *injuni*. They have lived in what are now called Rungwe and Kyela districts in the Great Rift Valley for at least 500 years.

The Haya in northwestern Tanzania near the border with Uganda, hundreds of miles away from the Nyakyusa, also call 'birds,' *njuni*.

The Kamba, even farther away in eastern Kenya, also call birds, *njuni*.

And there are probably others Bantus who also use the term *njuni* for birds.

All their languages belong to the Bantu linguistic group.

Ndalama or *indalama* means 'money' in Nyakyusa, while the Swahili term for 'money' is *fedha*. The Nyakyusa also call 'money,' *kyuma*.

But the exact term for money in Nyakyusa is *ndalama* or *indalama* depending on the context in which the word is used, while *kyuma* really means 'metal' or 'steel.' But it is also used figuratively, meaning 'money.'

The Nyakyusa term, *kyuma*, is almost identical to the Swahili word, *chuma*, which also means 'metal.'

Mbulukutu or *imbulukutu* means 'ear' or 'ears' in Kinyakyusa, or Nyakyusa. In Swahili, *sikio* means 'ear,' and *masikio* means 'ears.'

Nkulu gwangu means 'my elder brother' in Nyakyusa. In Swahili, it's *kaka yangu*.

Ndaga fijo in Nyakyusa means 'thank you very much.' In Swahili, *asante sana* means 'thank you very much.'

So, there are some differences in Bantu languages or languages of Bantu origin.

Yet similarities abound. For example, in Kiswahili, n*jia* means 'way' or 'path,' as opposed to 'road.' In Kinyakyusa, it is *njila*.

Swahili for 'chicken' is *kuku*; Nyakyusa – *nguku*.

Nyama means 'meat' in Swahili and Nyakyusa and in many other Bantu languages including Xhosa. The Nyakyusa also say *inyama*, meaning 'meat,' depending on the context in which the term is used.

Among the Nyakyusa, *imbututu* is a kind of very large black bird with red beaks which exists in real life and which I saw many times when I lived in Nyakyusaland; while among the Xhosa, *impundudu* is a mystical, huge lightning bird that is an integral part of their traditional beliefs.

And *mvua* means 'rain' in Swahili, while in Nyakyusa it's called *fula*.

In Sotho, also known as Southern Sotho spoken in Lesotho and South Africa especially in the Free State Province, the word for 'crocodile' is *koena*. In Nyakyusa language, 'crocodile' is *ngwina*. The two terms, *koena* and *ngwina*, sound pretty close.

Those are just some examples. There are many others in many other African languages as well.

All those terms cited here, in Nyakyusa and Swahili, have their counterparts with almost the same spelling and the same meaning in many other Bantu languages which differ from Most West African languages – such as Igbo, Yoruba, Ewe, Wolof, and Twi – in many respects although they all belong to the same Niger-Congo family.

Then there's the concept or philosophy of *ubuntu* as it is known in South Africa, a black African term.

Ubuntu is a belief or philosophy whose essence is the virtue of being humane....

The Nyakyusa and other Africans have the same belief, what black South Africans call *ubuntu*, but use different terms to define it. Yet there are striking similarities in the terms used among many of them.

While black South Africans say *ubuntu,* the Nyakyusa say *ubundu*, sometimes simply *bundu* depending on the context; hardly any difference even in linguistic terms between what black South Africans call *ubuntu* and what the Nyakyusa of Tanzania and Malawi call *ubundu* or *bundu*.

In Kiswahili, or Swahili, it is called *utu*.

All those linguistic and philosophical similarities clearly point to a common origin of these people and their languages as members of the Niger-Congo family who migrated from what is today central-eastern Nigeria and Cameroon about 2000 years ago and spread throughout East, Central and Southern Africa.

There are still more similarities. For example, according to studies done by British anthropologists Godfrey Wilson and Monica Wilson, who were husband and wife, the Venda of South Africa and the Ngonde-Nyakyusa of Tanzania and Malawi also have many strong cultural similarities.

Godfrey Wilson's study, *The Nyakyusa of South-Western Tanganyika*, is contained in a book, *Seven Tribes of Central Africa*, published in 1951.

And some of the best anthropological studies ever conducted in the field were done by Monica Wilson on the Nyakyusa and published as books, *Good Company: A Study of Nyakyusa Age-Villages*, and *Rituals of Kinship Among the Nyakyusa*, among other works by her on the Nyakyusa and other tribes in the region.

The Venda are also related to the Lemba of South Africa and Zimbabwe who, according to genetic (DNA) evidence, are also partly Jewish, tracing part of their heritage to Sena in Yemen more than 2,000 years ago.

But in spite of being partly Jewish, the Lemba are predominantly of Bantu stock, and their language is related to other Bantu languages in East, Central and Southern Africa.

The Lemba became part of the Venda community long after the Venda had settled in the region. They believe that they are Black Jews and descendants of the lost tribe of Israel. They usually keep to themselves and only marry within their own group.

They also sometimes refer to themselves as *Vhalungu*, which means 'non-Negroid' or 'respected foreigner.' But this is just a form of inferiority complex on their part, ashamed of what they are as black Africans.

Although they have some Jewish genes, they are mostly black African of 'Negro' stock or origin which some of them may despise so much; hence 'we respected foreigners.'

And there are a lot of things all these communities have in common as an African people. In fact many of these ethnic groups – or tribes – use identical terms in many cases to identify the same objects and natural phenomena.

It is from such linguistic similarities that the term 'Bantu' is derived to identify the people who speak these related languages. And the term 'Bantu' – or any other term similar to that – simply means 'people'; except that in this case the term 'Bantu' means 'these particular people' and not just any other people.

The term 'Bantu' – as a collective term used to identify the people mostly in East, Central and Southern Africa who speak related languages – was coined in the 1850s by W.H.I. Bleek, a librarian of the British government of the Cape Colony and has been used since then, although it had derogatory connotations during the apartheid era.

And because of its racist connotations in the past, most blacks in South Africa don't accept the term when it's used to identify them as a people or as individuals who are members of the Bantu family of ethnic groups. In fact, in the minds of most black South Africans, it's still a pejorative term even today.

But it is widely used in other parts of Africa – East and Central – without any problems to identify Bantu speakers. However, it must be emphasised that there is no Bantu race. 'Bantu' is, simply, a linguistic term more than anything else." – Godfrey Mwakikagile, *South Africa as a Multi-Ethnic Society*, Continental Press, Dar es Salaam, Tanzania, 2010, pp. 16 – 24, 26 – 28).

The word *vhalungu* used by the Lemba is very similar to Swahili's *wazungu* which means *whites* and to the Ngonde-Nyakyusa term *basungu* which means the same thing; not very much different from the meaning of the Lemba term *vhalungu* if used in an elastic sense simply to mean "non-black" or "foreigner" – not necessarily "respected foreigner."

I am also reminded of another similarity. When Emmerson Mnangagwa, "the Crocodile," was being cheered by tens of thousands of Zimbabweans after Robert Mugabe was ousted by the army and by popular uprising, some people were carrying signs saying, *ngwena*, and were chanting *ngwena*, meaning "crocodile" in Shona. That is almost exactly the same word the Ngonde-Nyakyusa use: *Ngwina* means "crocodile" in the Nyakyusa language.

Here is another similarity: *Harare*, a Shona word which is also the name of the capital of Zimbabwe, is *halali* in Swahili, meaning "he/she does not sleep." It means basically the same thing in Shona.

There are just as many linguistic similarities in the languages spoken by the member of different ethnic groups in Malawi.

It may be one of the smallest countries in Africa, but it is also a microcosm of the continent in many fundamental respects including history: free migration of the indigenous people from one part of Africa to another before the coming of Europeans who partitioned the continent. It is also a microcosm of the continent in terms of African identity, of the different ethnic groups which collectively constitute the one-ness of Africa, what Dr. Kwame Nkrumah called the African personality.

The culture

THE culture of Malawi is predominantly black African because the vast majority of the people are black.

Different cultures of different tribes or ethnic groups collectively constitute the culture of Malawi, although there really is no single culture for the country as a whole. There is no well-defined national culture except for some attributes derived from the cultures of various tribes which are shared by the vast majority of Malawians. And those attributes have a lot do with the common history and common origin of the people of Malawi hundreds of years ago.

Therefore the cultures of the different tribes or ethnic groups are not sub-cultures of one national culture. They are independent of each other as entities with their own individual identities. Yet they are united by what they have in common.

Still, different tribes have different customs and traditions. They also have different religious beliefs. Also their music is different and their dances are different even when they have some things in common.

There are also significant regional differences. People from the northern region have a reputation for being better educated and more skilled in business than their counterparts in the south and in other parts of the country. For this reason, they are mistrusted by people from the southern two-thirds of the country and efforts are made to keep them out of government positions.

They include the Tumbuka, and the Ngonde who are known as Nyakyusa in neighbouring Tanzania. Coincidentally, members of the Nyakyusa tribe in Tanzania are also some of the most highly educated people in that country together with the Chaga and the Haya.

The three tribes have virtually dominated Tanzania in terms of education since – and even before – independence. Tanzania has 126 tribes or ethnic groups, contrasted with Malawi which has only a few.

Malawi does not have a national dress. Men dress in a Western style, wearing shirts and trousers.

Women often wear traditional costumes consisting of two or three *chitenjes* – known in Kiswahili or Swahili as kitenge (singular) and vitenge (plural) in Tanzania. They are large pieces of coloured fabric used as a skirt, as a headdress, and as a sarong-like wrap that holds a small infant on the woman's back.

One way to distinguish between the three regions of Malawi – North, Central and South – is by the colour of the dress. Red, blue, and green represent the north, central, and southern regions, respectively.

Men dominate society as they do elsewhere across Africa. And gender roles are well-defined except in a few cases in urban areas where educated women have tried to break down gender barriers.

Still, men are in a privileged position, resulting in social inequalities. For example, historically, it is men who have had the opportunity to go to school, not only in Malawi but in other African countries. That was also the case during colonial rule.

Most of the educated people in Malawi or those who can read and write are men. At least 75 per cent of literate people are men.

Even when food is served, men come first. And usually, men eat separately from women, using the only table in the house. The woman serves the meal to the man, often on her knees. But that is mostly in the rural areas although the practice is not uncommon in towns and cities among Malawians who stick to tradition.

At weddings, it is customary for the bride to serve food to the husband's parents while on her knees as a sign of respect and submissiveness.

Marriages are often arranged by parents and other relatives such as uncles and aunts. That is mainly the case in the rural areas.

Dowries play a significant role in the selection of a partner. They are usually in the form of livestock such as cattle, goats and even chickens, but may consist of grain or land.

Larger women often are favoured as brides because they appear to come from a well-to-do family that can provide a significant dowry and seem strong enough to carry heavy loads.

Preference for large or fat women is common in many African societies. Female relatives even over-feed girls to fatten them and make them more attractive to men as prospective brides or future wives. Men also see them as being more beautiful and attractive than smaller or skinny or thin women.

Polygamy is still practised by a significant number of men especially those who can afford it. Sometimes the co-wives even share the same house with the husband.

But many people of the younger generation – both men and women – prefer monogamy and don't like polygamy.

Divorce is not uncommon. But it can be very hard on women because in many cases their families are reluctant to take them back. They are also required to return the dowry to the husband.

Also, after divorce, the husband is entitled to all property. He gets all the couple's possessions leaving nothing for his ex-wife.

But there is closeness in kinship that is not common in

some societies. Families are quite close and often live in adjoining houses. Elderly persons are taken care of by their children. Usually, the oldest members of a family have a strong voice in running the household and raising the children.

Especially important is the uncle. Male adolescents ask advice first of the uncle who is also influential in the selection of a bride.

The process of socialisation, training children to be responsible members of society, starts early as is the case in most traditional societies on the continent. Children are raised under strict family control, usually by the mother, until they leave home. And they are expected to help with the chores of daily living.

Most tasks are done by female children. Tasks include carrying water, cleaning the home, washing dishes, and going to the market to buy or sell a variety of items.

There is a strong emphasis on education. Half the population over the age of fifteen can read and write, but education is reserved for those who can afford it: school fees and uniforms. Most children have to end their education before high school to help tend the fields or care for younger siblings.

Like most Africans, Malawians welcome and help strangers. Any visitor is always offered a drink and something to eat. Eating usually is done only with the right hand. The left hand is considered "dirty."

A person approaching someone's house will often cry *Odi, Odi* to announce his or her presence. It sounds almost identical to the Swahili term, *hodi*, which means the same thing.

All that is part of *ubuntu*, a philosophy and way of life typical of traditional African societies. It emphasises hospitality, sharing, sympathy. What is mine is yours, and what is yours is mine. I am diminished as a human being when you are diminished and when any other human being is diminished. Your suffering is my suffering, and your joy is my joy.

That is the essence of *ubuntu*. Malawians, like other Africans, take it very seriously.

Another very important aspect of Malawian life is how funerals are conducted. Reverence for life includes a long period of mourning which can last for several days.

Life is generally short because of disease including the AIDS pandemic.

Modern medicine is available but traditional healers also play a very important role. Medicine men and women provide health care for many people, especially in the rural areas, using traditional or folk medicine. They use natural medicines such as roots, herbs, and potions.

Medicine men base their healing on the assumption that most illnesses are caused by supernatural powers and that supernatural powers are required to cure them.

The individual may fall ill after offending one of the gods, through witchcraft or sorcery, or through the unprovoked attack of an evil spirit.

The task of the curer is to diagnose the disease and then apply the spiritual remedy, such as retrieving a lost soul, removing a disease-causing object, or exorcising an evil spirit.

Often medicine men are called on to help in areas not considered medical problems in the West, such as finding a wife or a lover, conceiving a child, getting a job or a scholarship, and helping in business matters.

What this clearly shows is that, in spite of Western influence which has radically transformed Malawian society in many fundamental respects including availability of modern medicine, the traditional way of life is still very strong in Malawi. Even highly educated people including Christians go to traditional healers.

Customs and traditions remain the essence of the African way of life in Malawi. And no amount of foreign influence is going to change that.

Towns and Cities

MALAWI is one of the least urbanised countries in Africa. And it does not have large towns or cities even by African standards.

There are only four major urban centres in Malawi: Blantyre, Lilongwe, Zomba and Mzuzu.

More than any other urban centre in Malawi, Blantyre has attracted the largest number of people from all parts of the country for a variety of reasons.

It is the largest city in Malawi. It is the nation's financial and commercial centre. And it is the most cosmopolitan, with all the glitter and glamour associated with city life and cultural diversity.

It also has the widest range of opportunities across the spectrum among all the towns and cities in Malawi, attracting people from all walks of life, and in all fields, from the most humble to the most exalted.

In 2015, Blantyre had a population of more than 1 million, and still growing.

It is also contrasted with Lilongwe in one fundamental respect. While Lilongwe, as the nation's capital, is known as the political capital of Malawi, Blantyre is called Malawi's commercial capital and not just the nation's commercial centre. It is also the capital of the Southern Region and Blantyre District.

It is located in the Shire Highlands in the geographical

centre of the Southern Region.

The city is on the eastern edge of the Great Rift Valley. And because of that, some prominent faults occur within and in the vicinity of the city rendering it prone to earthquakes.

The main faults and associated zones of deeply fractured bedrock run from the north of the city in a south-westerly direction, and are potential acquifers for groundwater.

In terms of demographic composition, Blantyre is predominantly black. But there are significant numbers of whites mostly from England and other parts of Europe as well as South Africa. It has an expatriate population of more than 30,00, mostly British because of historical ties since Malawi, as Nyasaland, was once a British colony.

The Supreme Court of Malawi is located in Blantyre. And the Malawi Broadcasting Corporation (MBC) which is the nation's broadcaster and the provider of the country's only television channel is also based in Blantyre.

Blantyre is also an education centre with constituent colleges of the University of Malawi. Other academic institutions include the College of Medicine, the Kamuzu College of Nursing, Blantyre School of Health Sciences, Malawi Polytechnic, and the Malawi College of Accountancy. There are others.

Individual entrepreneurs provide specialised training in varied fields such as management, secretarial, business, accounting, and computers.

The city also has more schools than any other urban centre in Malawi.

Blantyre was founded in 1876 through the missionary work of the Church of Scotland. It is named after the town in South Lanarkshire, Scotland, where the explorer and missionary-doctor David Livingstone was born.

And its historical importance is rivalled by no other town or city in Malawi. It has many historic and cultural heritage resources which constitute a vital part of the city.

And they are very important to the city's identity. They include the Museum of Malawi.

They also constitute a vital part of the city's cultural and social wellbeing and are a powerful magnet attracting businesses. They have also helped to boost tourism through the years.

Blantyre is Malawi's oldest municipality and one of the oldest urban centres in East, Central and Southern Africa. It was built before Nairobi, Harare and Johannesburg and has the longest historic and cultural heritage in the region.

Blantyre also is the nation's main manufacturing centre. A variety of industries are based in the city, including shoe and cotton manufacturing. There are also metal and plastic-producing factories.

No other urban centre in Malawi can rival that. Blantyre stands out among all the nation's towns and cities as the industrial capital of the country.

It is also a transport communications node with road, rail and air links to all parts of the country and the neighbouring countries of Tanzania, Zambia, Mozambique, Zimbabwe and South Africa.

As the nation's commercial and industrial capital, Blantyre has a strong economic base for sustained economic growth. And its diversified economy offers a wide range of employment opportunities, attracting people from all parts of the country in search of better life. Its magnetic pull especially on the rural areas is irresistible, but also potential for disaster.

Uncontrolled population growth, an influx fuelled by dreams of good life in the city, may lead to urban unrest with dire consequences for the nation as a whole. Fortunately, Blantyre has not yet reached that point and has a chance to avert a catastrophe – an urban explosion which has rocked other countries in different parts of the Third World including Africa.

As a growing commercial centre, Blantyre has the potential capacity to absorb a significant number of people who continue to flock into the city. It has a strong economic sector since commerce, trade and industry – all based in Blantyre – collectively constitute a major component of the economy, second only to agriculture. This economic sector also has the greatest multiplier effect on the urban economy.

The informal sector also plays a very important role in the economic well-being of the city; a phenomenon common in other major urban centres across the continent where the subterranean economy, more often than not unregulated, is the primary source of income and means of livelihood for millions of people on the periphery of the mainstream.

A large population is a burden on the city in terms of service provision. One of those areas is health. But Blantyre still is the nation's best hope in terms of health care.

It has the biggest referral hospital in the country, Queen Elizabeth Central Hospital (QECH) which is run by the government. But the best hospital is run by the Seventh-Day Adventist Church (SDA). Blantyre Adventist Hospital and Mwaiwathu Private (PVT) Hospital are the best medical facilities in Malawi.

Following the liberalisation policy, the city has witnessed the establishment of many private clinics and hospitals. The majority of them offer out-patient services. And the few well-established ones offer both out-patient and in-patient services. Besides the city-based health services, many city residents make regular use of mission hospitals which are located outside the city.

Traditional healers (herbalists) and Traditional Birth Attendants (TBAs) also play an important role in providing health care to the city residents in the form of curative and maternal delivery services respectively.

The health delivery system of the city is grossly inadequate.

The public hospital wards are very congested and long

queues are characteristic of outpatients services.

The average clinic-population ratio for the city is between 25,000 and 28,000 persons per clinic, and the unplanned settlements are the least served with over 40,000 persons per clinic, compared with the recommended urban planning standard of 10,000 persons per clinic.

Mwaiwathu Private Hospital and Blantyre Adventist Hospital not only provide the best medical services in the city; they serve the whole country.

Many residents from the nation's capital Lilongwe – including high-raking government officials and their families – travel to Blantyre to receive treatment from the two hospitals. Also, other people from different parts of Malawi travel long distances to go to Blantyre and get treatment at these hospitals.

It is a searing indictment against the government. It has not done enough to provide adequate health care for its people the way private hospitals do. Even its referral hospital, Queen Elizabeth Central Hospital which is supposed to be the pride of the nation, is no match for them.

When people in Malawi talk about excellent medical service, they are talking about Blantyre Adventist Hospital and Mwaiwathu Private Hospital.

The two are synonymous with excellence in the medical field in Malawi.

And the city of Blantyre itself is synonymous with modern development in the context of Malawi even if many of its facilities are not necessarily among the best.

Next we look at Lilongwe.

Lilongwe, the nation's capital, is the largest city in Malawi. It had a population of 1,077,116 in 2015, slightly larger than Blantyre's of 1,068,681 during the same period.

Lilongwe became the capital in 1974, replacing Zomba.

Located in the Central Region, it is built on the banks

of the Lilongwe River near the border of Malawi, Mozambique and Zimbabwe.

Lilongwe had two advantages which made it the capital of Malawi: its central location; it is also in a region which is home to Malawi's first president, Ngwazi Dr. Hastings Kamuzu Banda.

But although it's the nation's capital, it has yet to reach the stature and status of the nation's commercial centre, Blantyre, which is also the economic hub of the south.

Lilongwe's population has grown very fast. It was approximately half of Blantyre's in 2006. And international business continues to look to Blantyre, not Lilongwe, for banking and commercial interests.

In terms of Lilongwe's demographic composition, besides black, a significant number of whites who live in the city also come from South Africa. Others are Europeans working for different organisations. The city has also attracted a large number of people from the rural areas seeking employment and better life. It is also under severe strain because of its rapid population growth.

Mzuzu is the third-largest city in Malawi and is the centre of an agricultural region. The areas around it produce tea, coffee and rubber.

It is also the capital of the Northern Region and had a population of 128,432 in 2016.

The coffee which is grown in the areas around Mzuzu is well-known for its high quality. And the tea grown in both the Northern and Southern regions of Malawi is recognised around the world as being among the finest on the market.

To the south of the city of Mzuzu is Viphya Forest, the largest man-made forest in Africa. And the area lists itself as containing the third-largest rain forest in the world.

To the northwest of the city is the Nyika National (Game) Park, Malawi's largest.

The grasslands of Nyika also have one of the highest densities of leopard in Central Africa.

Mzuzu is also home to Mzuzu University founded in 1994. Mzuzu Central Hospital is also located in the city. It's one of four such hospitals in Malawi.

Located 40 miles north of the commercial capital Blantyre is Zomba, the fourth-largest city in Malawi. It had a population of about 101,140 in 2009.

And it has a unique place in the country's history. During colonial times, it was the capital of British Central Africa, a protectorate established by the British in the area of present-day Malawi. The British Central Protectorate existed between 1891 and 1907.

Zomba then became the capital of Nyasaland before this colonial possession was renamed Malawi in 1964. And it remained the capital of independent Malawi for 10 years until 1974.

The city is also known for its British colonial architecture. The town's British colonial past is reflected in the architecture of its older buildings and homes. Zomba was once a hub for expatriates in Malawi. Its diverse cultural mix included British tobacco farmers and Dutch, German and American emissaries.

It is also home to Chancellor College of the University of Malawi. Chancellor College is the largest of the constituent colleges of the University of Malawi. The college has five faculties: the Faculty of Humanities, the Faculty of Science, the Faculty of Law, the Faculty of Social Science and the Faculty of Education.

Although the capital was moved north to Lilongwe after the end of colonial rule, Zomba still remained the seat of Parliament until 1994 when the government finally made the move complete.

Zomba is located at the foot of Zomba Mountain.

But there is a dispute on Zomba's status as the fourth-largest city in Malawi. Some statistics show it as the third-largest, and Mzuzu, the fourth-largest, depending on the source. According to one source, Mzuzu had a population of more than 80,000 in 2009 while Zomba had more

100,000 in the same year.

Although Malawi's large towns and cities are growing fast, a trend common across the continent because of economic forces driving millions of people, especially the youth, into urban areas, most of the people still live in the rural areas.

Also, it is only two cities, Blantyre and Lilongwe, which have grown the fastest and which have the strongest economic and social incentives drawing large numbers of people into those urban centres.

With a population of more than 18 million people in 2017, Malawi remains one of the least urbanised countries in Africa:

"It is urbanizing at a very rapid rate, however, with movement toward urban areas taking place at a pace far swifter than either the African or global averages.

A rural village – called a *mudzi* – is usually small. Organized around the extended family, it is limited by the amount of water and arable land available in the vicinity.

On the plateaus, which support the bulk of the population, the most common village sites are at the margins of *madambo*, which are usually contiguous with streams or rivers and are characterized by woodland, grassland, and fertile alluvial soils.

In highland areas, scattered villages are located near perennial mountain streams and pockets of arable land.

The larger settlements of the Lake Malawi littoral originated in the 19th century as collection points for slaves and later developed as lakeside ports. Improvements in communications and the sinking of wells in semiarid areas permitted the establishment of new settlements in previously uninhabited areas.

Architecture is changing: the traditional round, mud-walled, grass-roofed hut is giving way to rectangular brick buildings with corrugated iron roofs....

Although some district centres and missionary stations

have an urban appearance, they are closely associated with the rural settlements surrounding them....

The population is growing at a rate above average for sub-Saharan Africa. The birth rate is among the highest on the continent, but the death rate is also high, and life expectancy for both genders is significantly lower than the average for sub-Saharan Africa, primarily because of the incidence of HIV/AIDS." – (Malawi, *Encyclopaedia Britannica*, 2017).

Urban residents are some of the people who have been most affected by the AIDS pandemic. Still, Malawi's towns and cities, as those of other countries across Africa, remain vibrant centres of economic activities. But it is the agricultural sector which is the backbone of Malawi's economy. The manufacturing sector, which is urban-centred, is extremely small, a phenomenon common across the continent.

The mining sector is negligible. There are hardly any minerals which can be exploited in commercial quantities. Tourism is more important than mining.

But that could change if large quantities of petroleum – as they are believed to be – are discovered in Lake Nyasa. However, exploitation of oil reserves in the lake faces major obstacles, one being environmental concerns. There is fear that drilling and extraction of oil could result in massive pollution. It will be an environmental disaster destroying fish and other forms of life as well as means of livelihood millions of people who live around and near the lake depend on. It is not just Malawians who will be affected but Tanzanians and Mozambicans as well.

There is also the dispute with Tanzania over the lake that has not been resolved. Tanzania is going to claim a share of the oil reserves in the aprt of the lake she contends is an integral part of Tanzanian territory.

The future of Malawi as a small and poor country will probably depend on the extent to which this landlocked nation strengthens economic ties with the countries in the region that are members of the Southern African Development Community (SADC), of which she is one. Her future may also lie in the revival of the federation that once existed as a union of Nyasaland, Southern Rhodesia, and Northern Rhodesia but which will now serve the interests of the majority of the people unlike in the past when white minorities ruled those countries.

But formation of such a federation is sheer speculation and is a remote possibility at best.

Printed in Great Britain
by Amazon